"So often, I find it is a struggle to make a [...] relatable to kids. But Christie Thomas has done exactly that in *Fruit Full: 100 Family Experiences for Growing in the Fruit of the Spirit*. By combining Bible stories with some of her own personal adventures, Thomas has created a resource that is both biblically sound and fun to read. She goes beyond explanations to encourage children to look for the Spirit's fruits in their own lives, as well as to seek a deeper connection with Christ. With just the right amount of humor to keep kids engaged, *Fruit Full* is sure to be a sweet experience for your family's devotion time."
—Tama Fortner, award-winning author of more than forty books, including *Simply Christmas: A Busy Mom's Guide to Reclaiming the Peace of the Holidays*

"Christie Thomas's approach to helping children grow in Christ exhibits everything you'd want in a devotional: depth, warmth, and surprising insights."
—Marianne Hering, author of the Adventures in Odyssey®: The Imagination Station® series

"In this devotional, Christie does a fabulous job of making big virtues accessible to little people. This guide is practical and relational—easy enough for a tired parent at the end of the day, but deep enough to produce real conversation and a better understanding of who Christ is and who he has created us to be."
—Danielle Hitchen, author of the Baby Believer® series

"Christie Thomas provides a tremendous resource for families. . . . Through this kid-friendly, comprehensive study, children will learn how to be rooted in Jesus in order to experience continual spiritual growth."
—Crystal Bowman, best-selling, award-winning author of more than 100 books for children, including *Our Daily Bread for Kids*, and *I Love You to the Stars: When Grandma Forgets, Love Remembers*

"Would you like the fruit of the Spirit to be a reality in your children's lives and your family life? Pick up this outstanding book and let it guide you!"
—Diane Stortz, author of *I AM: 40 Reasons to Trust God*

FRUIT FULL

100 FAMILY EXPERIENCES FOR GROWING IN THE FRUIT OF THE SPIRIT

CHRISTIE THOMAS

KREGEL
PUBLICATIONS

Fruit Full: 100 Family Experiences for Growing in the Fruit of the Spirit
© 2022 by Christie Thomas

Published by Kregel Publications, a division of Kregel Inc., 2450 Oak Industrial Dr. NE, Grand Rapids, MI 49505.

The author is represented by the literary agency of Credo Communications, LLC, Grand Rapids, Michigan, www.credocommunications.net.

Cover art and illustrations © Luke Flowers

ISBN 978-0-8254-4728-0, print
ISBN 978-0-8254-7776-8, epub
ISBN 978-0-8254-6929-9, Kindle

Printed in the United States of America
22 23 24 25 26 27 28 29 30 31 / 5 4 3 2

To the one
who feels like you're always striving
and never growing:
may you find freedom
in Christ.

CONTENTS

LETTER TO PARENTS

But the Holy Spirit produces this kind of fruit in our lives: love,
joy, peace, patience, kindness, goodness, faithfulness, gentleness,
and self-control. There is no law against these things!
(GALATIANS 5:22–23)*

Dear Parent,

We don't know each other, but I think we probably are more alike than
we realize. Have you ever tried to become more patient? I tried to grow in
patience for years, and I discovered something about God along the way. He
does give sudden supernatural patience . . . occasionally. But more often, he
gives us a child whose tantrums get on our last nerve.

Oh, was that just me?

Maybe you've tried to become more gentle and kind, only to have a child
who asks for snacks 80 million times a day, causing your brittle temper to
crack and your words to spill out, unkind and ungentle. Or maybe that was
just me too.

Sometimes it seems like growing spiritually is like trying to roll out pizza
dough. I squash it with my rolling pin only to have it snap back to its original
shape. I roll it again and it snaps back again, but this time it's a little bit wider. It
takes a lot of tugging and rolling to get that pizza dough to conform to the pan.

Growing spiritually is similar because we tend to grow a bit, then snap
back—like that elastic pizza dough. Then the Lord tugs and rolls our souls
again, and we grow a little . . . only to ooze inward once more.

---

* All Scriptures are quoted from the New Living Translation unless otherwise specified because I personally find this translation to be the most accessible to children. Feel free to look up
each passage in your preferred translation before or after reading the devotion.

But it's worth letting him work in us, kneading and growing and rolling our souls, because in the end, the pizza he's making is a life of love, joy, peace, patience, kindness, goodness, faithfulness, gentleness, and self-control. (Maybe with a mushroom garnish.)

The key is that *God* does the rolling, tugging, and growing, usually by giving us situations that force us to depend on him. And this applies to our children's growth as well. Alas, my pizza dough spiritual growth analogy isn't in the Bible, but there's another one that is: the fruit of the Spirit.

THE FRUITY PROBLEM

In my more than twenty years in children's ministry, I often used curricula that turned the fruit of the Spirit into character traits we wanted to see in our kids. We labeled apples and bananas with permanent markers and gave them grape-scented stickers and magnets, but kids just didn't understand. Worse, they didn't grow spiritually. Finally, I figured out why.

The fruit of the Spirit isn't a to-do list.

Training our kids to do better at each fruit of the Spirit isn't Christian because the fruits of the Spirit aren't just nice character traits to practice. They are evidence of a life that is crucified with Christ and living in the resurrection power of his Spirit. They're fruit, not rules.

Training kids to obey God without also telling them about the hope of Christ will either create moralistic children or make them rebel. Just ask the ancient Israelites. They were given law, and they rebelled until they lost their land. Then they turned into legalistic Pharisees, adding to the law until it was an incredible burden on everyone.

The law is not the Christian way. The gospel is the Christian way.

But what is the gospel?

The gospel is the good news of how God sees you and treats you. Not only did God make you, he adores you. But you (and everyone else on this planet) have sinned. It breaks the relationship between you and God because he is holy. God's holiness and your sinfulness are like oil and water. They just don't mix. God fixed it from his end by coming as a man to remove the power of sin over us through his death and resurrection. He invites you into relationship with him. Your job is to believe in his love. Accept his forgiveness, then put your hand in his and let him help you choose love every day.

The gospel brings so much freedom—to our kids and us. It frees us from the expectation that they'll behave well (because honestly, they're sinners, just like us!) and it reminds us to depend on God for our goodness.

Just like we can't tell an apple tree to try harder to bear fruit, we can't tell our kids to try harder to bear spiritual fruit. No one can force themselves to love more—at least, not on the inside. To be truly transformed into more loving people, we need to be changed from the inside out.

Therefore, writing the word *love* on an apple won't help kids actually grow that fruit of the Spirit (or even truly understand what it is). Even making our kids memorize verses about love or make goals to be more loving is unlikely to help them grow the fruit of love. Any growth they do experience is outward obedience instead of true heart transformation.

SO HOW DO WE GROW IN THE FRUITS?

When Paul wrote about the fruit of the Spirit, he was giving us a metaphor for true life change. We are like plants, and to grow good fruit, we need to be rooted in God's love for us. Jesus said he is the Living Water and the Light of the World, so when we spend time with him, our lives grow and change, just as if we were plants with proper watering and sunshine. Then, like a tree, we will grow good fruit. And the good fruit that grows in our lives as a result of being with Christ is love, joy, peace, patience, kindness, goodness, faithfulness, gentleness, and self-control.

The fruit of the Spirit is evidence of a soul that is growing in Christ.

God is all the fruits rolled into one amazing, all-powerful being who cares for you and your child with a fierce, eternal love. "God in all his fullness was pleased to live in Christ" (Colossians 1:19), meaning that "Christ is the visible image of the invisible God" (Colossians 1:15). Jesus is all of God's attributes displayed in a single human being, which is why we're going to spend most of this devotional studying Jesus.

There won't be any hacks here, no "tips and tricks to make your child be good." Our kids will only be good when they fall in love with the good God who loves them enough to die for them. He covers them with his goodness and gives them his Spirit to help them grow a beautiful character that reflects Jesus.

John 15:5–8 reminds us that the only way to grow good fruit in our lives is to live deeply connected with Jesus, every day.

"Yes, I am the vine; you are the branches. Those who remain in me, and I in them, will produce much fruit. For apart from me you can do nothing. Anyone who does not remain in me is thrown away like a useless branch and withers. Such branches are gathered into a pile to be burned. But if you remain in me and my words remain in you, you may ask for anything you want, and it will be granted! When you produce much fruit, you are my true disciples. This brings great glory to my Father."

The book you're holding centers around this concept: that as we spend more time with Jesus, connected to the vine, we will grow in the fruit of the Spirit. The fruits then will naturally grow because they are the evidence of a life rooted in Christ. Each of the one hundred devotions will help kids see the fruit of the Spirit through the hands, heart, and habits of Jesus. As children connect with him, the Holy Spirit will change their own hands, hearts, and habits to be more like Christ.

HOW TO USE THIS BOOK

Over the next one hundred devotions, you'll discover the fruits of the Spirit as seen in the life and teachings of Jesus Christ. Each day, your family will

- explore a Christ-centered Bible passage and short devotional;
- start a fruitful conversation using the suggested discussion starter; and
- engage in a meaningful prayer that will help you draw closer to Jesus.

Each ten-devotion section also opens with ten simple, hands-on activities you can incorporate into your days to help your kids connect deeper with each aspect of Christ's character. Feel free to use those activities any time or not at all. Please visit fruitofthespiritbook.com for Bible verse printables and other activities.

For an Easter-focused thirty-day devotional, read the last three devotions in each fruit section. If you start on Ash Wednesday and read every weekday, you'll be done just before Easter.

THE FRUIT OF THE SPIRIT

HANDS-ON GROWTH ACTIVITIES

Use these activities as a hands-on supplement to the daily devotions. You can add in one per day, flip to this page for an idea only on days when you have a few extra minutes, or use a few of the activities each Sunday.

Memorize it: Memorize Galatians 5:22–23 together over the next two weeks.

Write it: Write out the memory verse. Use fun lettering and hang it somewhere obvious.

Draw it: If you were a tree, what would you look like? Draw yourself as a tree, bursting with good fruit.

Pray it: Pray a breath prayer: As you breathe in, say, "Be in me . . ." And as you breathe out, say, "and produce good fruit."

Research it: How is Psalm 1 similar to the idea of the fruit of the Spirit?

Imagine it: Pretend to be a tiny seed. Imagine that it's raining on you, and then the sun is shining. Stretch up and grow into a beautiful tree!

Play it: Plant a real seed or even a tree. Watch it grow over the next few weeks as you read about the various ways we are like plants.

Sing it: Find a song about the fruit of the Spirit (or make up your own).

Ask it: Why does God care that we grow good fruit in our lives?

Speak it: Grab a piece of yummy fruit and hold it up in the air as you recite the memory verse.

For Bible verse printables and other activities,
please visit fruitofthespiritbook.com.

DAY 1

WHAT IS THE FRUIT OF THE SPIRIT?

But the Holy Spirit produces this kind of fruit in our lives: love,
joy, peace, patience, kindness, goodness, faithfulness, gentleness,
and self-control. There is no law against these things!
(GALATIANS 5:22–23)

Have you ever planted a seed? It's fun to watch, but you can't just put a tomato seed on your kitchen table and expect it to magically produce juicy tomatoes. The seed needs certain things in order to grow.

Near the end of winter, my boys and I love to plant tomato seeds in tiny little pots on our kitchen windowsill. We tuck them gently into the soil, which will hold their roots in place and provide the food they need to grow.

Next, we give them water. Not too much, or they'll float away like a bug in a creek. They need just enough water to make the seeds swell up and crack open.

The most exciting part is when each stem breaks through the soil. It starts out curled up, then straightens and lifts its new leaves toward the sun like praying hands.

Eventually, we take the seedlings out of their little pots and replant them in the garden. They get a little annoyed at this and refuse to grow for a bit. But once they start, they don't stop.

After lots of rain and sun, small yellow flowers turn into delicious tomato fruits.

Do you like to eat fresh tomatoes? I take a big bite and let red juice dribble down my chin. Perhaps you like to enjoy them on a juicy hamburger instead.

Did you know you and I are like plants?

In this book, we're going to talk about the things we need in order to grow fruit in our lives and what the fruit looks like. You and I won't grow tomatoes out of our ears (thankfully!), but instead, we grow a different kind of fruit when we follow Jesus and let the Holy Spirit work in our hearts. The Bible calls this "the fruit of the Spirit." What are these fruits? They are love, joy, peace, patience, kindness, goodness, faithfulness, gentleness, and self-control. Those sound wonderful, don't they?

A healthy tomato fruit is proof my plant has received the right amount of nutrients, water, and sun. In the same way, the fruit of the Spirit is proof our hearts have received the right amount of God's Spirit, and we're becoming more like Jesus.

Are you ready to grow?

DISCUSSION STARTER

- Picture a tree in your mind. What helps this tree grow big and strong? Can a tree force itself to grow fruit?
- If your life is like a tree, what helps you grow more of the fruit of the Spirit?
- Which fruits of the Spirit do you want to grow?

PRAYER

God, please work in our hearts so we can become more like you. Please give us your Spirit so we can grow in love, joy, peace, patience, kindness, goodness, faithfulness, gentleness, and self-control. Amen.

DAY 2

TO BE FRUITFUL, WE NEED JESUS

"Yes, I am the vine; you are the branches. Those who remain in
me, and I in them, will produce much fruit. For apart from me
you can do nothing."
(JOHN 15:5)

Have you ever picked a flower, then tried to plant it at home? In case you
haven't, here's a tip: it won't grow because it is dead. It might not look dead,
and it might even look lovely in a vase on your kitchen table for a few days.
But you can be sure it will go from fresh to funky smelling very quickly.

It's the same with trying to grow the fruit of the Spirit all on our own.
Becoming more loving, patient, and kind on our own is like a picked flower
trying to turn into fruit. It's impossible.

Today's verse reminds us of the most important thing we need in order to
produce much fruit: Jesus.

Jesus was the only person in the world who had all the fruits of the Spirit
all the time. Jesus was full of love, joy, peace, patience, kindness, goodness,
faithfulness, gentleness, and self-control, and because of this, people loved to
be with him!

Sometimes we think in order to be more like Jesus, we just have to study
him and copy him. Jesus touched a leper? OK, I'll go touch a sick person.
Jesus fed five thousand people?

Um . . . that one's a little tricky.

Unfortunately, we can't become like Jesus by literally copying him. Instead,
Jesus says we need to remain in him.

We can remain in bed on a cozy Saturday morning, but how can we remain
in Jesus?

Here's how we remain in Jesus: we connect with him every day.

First, we connect with him when we're alone by praying and reading the Bible. You might not be able to read the Bible yet, but you can talk to God anytime you want.

Then, we connect with him as a family when we read the Bible, memorize verses, or pray together. That's what we're doing right now. High five!

Last, we connect with him in community when we go to church and serve together.

When we connect with Jesus every day, we remain in him. Then Jesus's Spirit, also called the Holy Spirit, hangs out with us, and it's his power that makes us more like him. The Holy Spirit actually changes us to become more like Jesus. Without him, we can't do it.

DISCUSSION STARTER

- Pick one specific way you can connect with Jesus each day—maybe reading this devotional or praying before bed. What time of day will you do it? How will you remember? (You can also decide on this as a family instead of as individuals.)

PRAYER

Jesus, you are the vine and we are the branches. Thank you that we don't have to do this Christian life in our own power. Teach us to remain in you and to connect with you every day. Amen.

DAY 3

HOW DO WE GROW GOOD FRUIT?

By his divine power, God has given us everything we need for
living a godly life. We have received all of this by coming to
know him, the one who called us to himself by means of his
marvelous glory and excellence.
(2 PETER 1:3)

Do you ever feel a lie fly out of your mouth like a nasty bug? That happens to
me sometimes. I'll be talking and a lie will slip out. It seems weird to be an
adult Christian who still lies at times. And yet, I do.

Maybe you don't have a problem with lying, but you boss your little sister
around a lot, or you have a grumpy attitude. Maybe you have cheated, or
taken something that wasn't yours, or been selfish. You know what? We all
have. All those bad choices we make are called *sin*. Anyone who says they
never sin is flat-out lying. Except Jesus. He was the only human ever who
never sinned.

Paul, one of Jesus's most famous followers, wrote in Romans 7:19, "I want
to do what is good, but I don't. I don't want to do what is wrong, but I do it
anyway."

When Jesus died, he offered forgiveness for all those bad choices we make.
But that doesn't mean we turn into perfect people overnight. Even when
you're a Christian, sin can sometimes feel like a monster in your stomach
trying to tear its way out.

The verse we read today says we have everything we need for living a
godly life. Imagine that all these godly living things are in a backpack you
carry around with you. What's in your backpack?

You might have some snacks and a good book or two. You'll need a Bible
for sure, but beyond that, who knows? A journal? A skateboard? A pair of
fuzzy slippers?

Thankfully, God has given us everything we need for godliness, and it's not a backpack full of fuzzy slippers. God has given us forgiveness through Jesus, and through the Holy Spirit he gives us the ability to say NO to sin and YES to things that help us live a godly life. The Holy Spirit helps us in those times when the sin monster wants to tear its way out. When we ask the Holy Spirit for help, he's right there, ready to smash that monster down to size and give us the power to choose what is right.

DISCUSSION STARTER

- What is one sin you feel like you can't stop doing? Let's bring our sins to God and ask him for the power to get rid of them from our lives.

PRAYER

Thank you, God, for forgiving us and also for changing us to be more like you. Holy Spirit, thank you for your power. Please change us to become more like Jesus! Amen.

DAY 4

THE FRUIT OF LIGHT

So now there is no condemnation for those
who belong to Christ Jesus.
(ROMANS 8:1)

Have you ever picked up a piece of rotten fruit? You might grab an orange
only to have your thumb squish right through the peel. It may have looked
good on top, but it was covered in green fur on the bottom. Blech. Rotten
pears have brown, squidgy spots all over them, and if you bite in without
noticing, you'll get a mouthful of mold.

Rotten fruit is good for nothing. You can't eat it, turn it into jam, or feed it
to your dog. It's only good for the compost heap.

We've been talking about the good fruit we grow when we're connected
to Jesus, but the Bible tells us that people can have bad fruit too. Quarrelling,
jealousy, outbursts of anger, selfishness, envy, and greediness are all bad
fruit. They may look good on the outside, but they'll rot your heart from the
inside. (You can read Galatians 5:19–21 if you want a nice, long list of bad
fruits.) Those bad fruits will grow in a person who has their spiritual roots in
the kingdom of darkness.

The great news is that God "has rescued us from the kingdom of darkness
and transferred us into the Kingdom of his dear Son, who purchased our
freedom and forgave our sins" (Colossians 1:13–14). God has adopted you into
his kingdom.

However, it's not always easy to go from darkness into light. Imagine you've
been adopted as a child of an important king. It would take a while for you to
learn how to act like a prince or princess, right? You would have to learn how
to bow and which fork to use at meals, how to make good decisions and which
advisors to listen to. It's the same with God's kingdom. You've been adopted
into his kingdom, but it takes a while to learn how to act like a child of God.

Even though we mess up and sometimes have more bad fruit than fruit of the Spirit, God says "there is no condemnation for those who belong to Christ Jesus" (Romans 8:1). No condemnation means God doesn't get angry with us when we make a bad choice.

We grow in the fruit of the Spirit because God slowly takes over all the dark parts of our hearts and shines his light on them. He cleans us up and helps us make better choices as we keep growing closer to him.

DISCUSSION STARTER

- What comes to mind when I say "kingdom of darkness" or "kingdom of light"?
- Tell me about a time you felt like a rotten person. How does Jesus see you?

PRAYER

Thank you, God, for bringing us into your kingdom of light and for not condemning us when we mess up. Help us to grow the fruit of the Spirit, not the fruit of darkness! Amen.

DAY 5

WHY SHOULD I BOTHER?

Well then, should we keep on sinning so that God can show us
more and more of his wonderful grace? Of course not! Since we
have died to sin, how can we continue to live in it?
(ROMANS 6:1–2)

We've been talking a lot about growing the fruit of the Spirit, and I wonder if
you've secretly had this question: "Why should I even want to grow the fruit
of the Spirit? It's a lot easier to just do whatever I want."

You wouldn't be the first person to ask that question. The first Christians
thought about this too. In fact, some people thought that since God forgives
us, it doesn't matter how we live our lives, like we can keep sinning because
God will keep forgiving us.

Imagine you have always lived on the streets, and the only way you can
survive is by stealing. You sleep in a cardboard box with someone's old jacket
as a blanket, and you rummage through garbage cans to find food. Then one
day the King decides to adopt you as his child. Incredible! You are taken back
to his palace, given royal robes, a canopy bed, and all the snacks you could
ever dream of. But along with your new life, you have to start acting like a
child of the King. You need to learn to be a protector, leader, and helper of
the King's people.

Now imagine you don't want to live like that, so you run away to live on
the streets again. You would still be the King's child, but you wouldn't be
acting like one. You wouldn't get the perks of living as a child of the King,
and the King's people won't get the protector, leader, and helper they need.

Jesus talked a lot about the kingdom of God, and he wasn't talking about
heaven. The kingdom of God is here, now, and we get to be part of it. You
and I are God's children, and it's our job to protect, lead, and help others, but
God needs to change us in order for us to do a good job. God doesn't want to

change us so we can be obedient little robots, roving around the world doing his bidding. He wants to change us so we can change the world through his love.

When God changes you to be more loving, joyful, peaceful, patient, kind, good, faithful, gentle, and self-controlled, you are able to become the person God created you to be.

DISCUSSION STARTER

- What's something that seems easier to do in the moment but always has consequences afterward?
- What do you imagine when you think of the kingdom of God?

PRAYER

God, thank you for saving us and giving us the gift of the Holy Spirit to help us follow you. Thank you for forgiving us. Please help us not to take your gift for granted but to follow you with all our hearts. Amen.

DAY 6

THE RIGHT FOOD

Jesus replied, "I am the bread of life. Whoever comes to me will
never be hungry again."
(JOHN 6:35)

A few years ago, I planted an apple tree. The first year, it grew six of the most delicious apples I had ever tasted. The next year, the tree grew a little taller and gave twelve delicious apples. I was hopeful that the next year I would have twenty delicious apples.

Except . . . it didn't have *any* apples the next year! Or the next. Or the next. I was so confused. My tree was growing taller and stronger, so it should have been growing fruit.

Finally, I talked to a tree expert.

As it turns out, I had been giving my tree the completely wrong fertilizer! The fertilizer I was giving it was perfect for growing nice leafy branches, but didn't give the tree what it needed to flower. It was getting the wrong food.

The tree expert told me to stop giving the tree the wrong food, and start giving it the right food.

So what does that have to do with Jesus? Well, in the verse above, Jesus said he is bread. If this sounds a little gross to you, you wouldn't be the only one to think so! After Jesus said this, a lot of people stopped following him because it was so confusing. Did he want people to nibble his ears or chomp his toes for dinner?

Thankfully, Jesus didn't mean we should eat a big slice of Jesus bread for lunch each day—he's not food for our stomachs! But there's another part of you that needs food, and it's called your soul. Your soul can't be seen on an X-ray or with a microscope, but it's part of you. If you were stuck in a hospital bed and couldn't move or talk or even breathe on your own, you would still have your soul, so you'd still be you. So, while food is important for our bodies, it is even more important that we feed our souls, because your soul is the part of you that will be with God forever.

Jesus is the *right* food for our souls. We often try to give our souls the wrong kind of food, just like I was giving my tree the wrong kind of food, but only Jesus will help us grow.

If we want our souls to grow and produce the fruit of the Spirit, we need to feast on Jesus. Feasting on Jesus doesn't mean eating him. It means we need him, just like we need food.

Oh, and my tree? A couple years later it gave me baskets and baskets of apples. All because I gave it the right food.

DISCUSSION STARTER

- How can we, as a family, feast on Jesus?
- How can you feast on Jesus on your own?

PRAYER

Thank you, Jesus, for being the food our souls need. Help us learn to feast on you and your words so we can grow healthy and strong. Amen.

DAY 7

THE STRONGEST ROOTS

Then Christ will make his home in your hearts as you trust in
him. Your roots will grow down into God's love and keep you
strong. And may you have the power to understand, as all
God's people should, how wide, how long, how high,
and how deep his love is.
(EPHESIANS 3:17–18)

Have you ever planted a seed in a piece of wet paper towel and watched it
grow? The very first thing to come out of that seed is a single root. It looks
kind of funny as it comes out, because it wiggles around like a worm, searching for soil and water. This tiny root-worm knows that water comes from
below, so no matter which way you plant your seed, the root will always end
up pointing down. If you plant the seed upside down, the root will go around
the seed so it can head down as soon as possible. A seed's roots can always
find water. God created seeds that way.

A seed doesn't need us to put an arrow next to it to show it the way to the
soil. Can you imagine all the tiny little arrow signs we would need to make
for all the seeds in the world? Thankfully, the root knows exactly what to do.
After the first little root settles into the soil, other roots grow out of the first
root. They spread out in order to find water and nutrients but also to keep
the growing plant from toppling over. The roots help the plant stand strong.

We are like these seeds. God has created us to seek out his love like a root
seeks out water. Last time, we learned that your soul is the part of you that
thinks and has feelings and will be with God forever. Close your eyes and
imagine your soul having little roots shooting out, seeking out love. When
they grow deep into God's love, your soul will grow strong.

What does that even mean? Well, in order to love God more, you need to
understand how much God loves you. When you get ignored, God's love can

remind you that he always sees you and you are precious. When you make a mistake, God's love reminds you that you don't have to be perfect; he loves you because you are his child, not because you're a good person. Trusting that God loves you, no matter what, will help you be more loving to yourself and to others.

To really understand God's love, we need to spend time with God, letting him show us his love. Ask him to show you how much he loves you. I think you might be surprised!

DISCUSSION STARTER

- How has God shown his love to you?
- Sometimes we look for love somewhere else instead of from God. Where else do people look for love?

PRAYER

God, thank you for your love that's so wide and long and high and deep that we can't ever be away from it. Please help our spiritual roots grow down into your love so our faith can grow strong. Give us the power to understand your incredible, earth-changing love. Amen.

DAY 8

THE BRIGHTEST LIGHT

Jesus spoke to the people once more and said, "I am the light of
the world. If you follow me, you won't have to walk in darkness,
because you will have the light that leads to life."
(JOHN 8:12)

A long time ago, I spent a night at someone else's home. They lived far out in
the country where there were no street lights, so it was much darker than I
was used to. In the middle of the night, I had to get up to use the washroom,
but there was a noisy thunderstorm outside. I held out my hands and felt my
way along the wall to the bathroom, letting my fingers guide me.

On the way back from the bathroom, my fingers guided me back to the
door of my bedroom. Suddenly, there was a huge CRASH and a bolt of lightning lit up the room. A ghostly white face stared right back at me from the
doorway! I cringed and screeched and my husband came running. When he
popped out of the room, I realized I wasn't actually standing in front of the
door. Nope, I was standing in front of a mirror! The ghostly face that had
terrified me was my own.

It's hard to get somewhere in the pitch dark, isn't it? I tried to use my fingers to guide me, but I got lost.

Just like my eyes needed light in order to help me navigate, plants need
light in order to grow. They use that light to make food, which helps plants
grow. I'm so glad they do this, because they create air for us to breathe and
food to eat.

Light is important both to help us find our way and to help us grow. But
did you know Jesus called himself "the light of the world"? This doesn't mean
Jesus has a glowing head or has flashlights for eyes (although that would be
a really handy superpower).

Here's what it means for Jesus to be the light of the world: he helps us see the world properly. He helps us see the difference between truth and lies, right and wrong, love and hate.

As the light, he also helps us grow strong spiritually. We don't want to be spiritual babies forever. We want to grow in wisdom and understanding and love, so we can eventually bear the kind of good fruit Paul calls "the fruit of the Spirit."

DISCUSSION STARTER

- Give some examples of how light helps you in your life.
- How does Jesus help you in your life?

PRAYER

Thank you, Jesus, for being the light of the world. Thank you for helping us see the difference between truth and lies, right and wrong, and love and hate. Please help us to grow by shining your light on our lives! Amen.

DAY 9

THE WETTEST WATER

Jesus replied, "Anyone who drinks this water will soon become thirsty again. But those who drink the water I give will never be thirsty again. It becomes a fresh, bubbling spring within them, giving them eternal life."
(JOHN 4:13–14)

One summer I went on vacation and left my tomato plants. I didn't realize what would happen if they didn't get watered for a few hot summer days, and when I came back, they looked like wilted lettuce. Oops! The next time I went on vacation, I got smart and left all my tomato pots in a kiddie pool full of water so they wouldn't dry out. It was a tomato pool party! When we returned, my kids swam in the shade of the happy tomato plants.

Our bodies need water too, just like plants. But unlike plants, we need two kinds of water: physical, refreshing, sloshing water to drink (preferably in lemonade form) and *living water*. Just like our souls need the right food (Jesus) and light (again, Jesus), we need living water (which is—you guessed it—Jesus).

We're all thirsty for Jesus, but most people don't know it. We think we're thirsty for money or popularity or being the smartest. Because we don't know we're actually thirsty for Jesus, we make bad choices. When we think we're thirsty for money, we might steal, cheat, or lie to get more money. When we think we're thirsty for popularity, we might hurt some really nice kids so we can be friends with the popular kids. When we think we're thirsty for being the smartest, we might become proud and rude to those who aren't as smart as us, or become jealous of those who are smarter.

Thankfully, it doesn't surprise Jesus when we try to fill our soul-thirst with other things.

He once met a woman at a well. She thought she was thirsty for human love, so she had gotten married five times. But Jesus knew she was actually thirsty for God's love, which is what he offered her. He called it living water. Once she understood what he was offering, she was so excited that she left her jar at the well and raced back to town to tell everyone!

Just like my tomato plants needed physical water to live well, we need Jesus's living water to live well. We need life with God.

DISCUSSION STARTER

- Most people don't know they are thirsty for God. Even Christians can get mixed up sometimes! Tell about a time you wanted something else more than you wanted God's love.

PRAYER

Jesus, you promised that when we drink the water you give, we will never thirst again. Please help us to feel thirsty for you so we actually want to know you more. Amen.

DAY 10

THE TOUGHEST PRUNING

"I am the true grapevine, and my Father is the gardener. He cuts
off every branch of mine that doesn't produce fruit,
and he prunes the branches that do bear fruit
so they will produce even more."
(JOHN 15:1–2)

Pruning plants seems kind of strange because it means cutting off parts of the plant. But without pruning, tomato plants can get sick or attract pests. Also, pruning tomato plants is the best way to get nice, big fruit earlier in the season!

So here's your Quick-and-Sneaky Guide to Pruning Tomatoes:

1. Find a tomato plant. That's always helpful when pruning tomatoes!
2. Look for its main stem. It's usually growing straight up.
3. Look for a leaf on the main stem. Right between the leaf and the stem you'll see a small stem, called a sucker. Get rid of that sucker! If it's little, you can pick it off with your fingernails. If it's big, you'll need some snippers.
4. Bonus: Yell "sayonara sucker!" as you pinch it off.

You might be imagining little plant screams right now: "Don't prune me! I'm impoooooortant!" Don't listen to it. Pruning your tomato plant will help it grow healthy and strong and give you lots of enormous tomatoes. If you let those little stems talk you into leaving them be, your plant will grow lots of leaves and only a few fruits. How sad. (Unless you don't like tomatoes.)

This is the pruning process Jesus was talking about in the verses we read today. Did you know that you and I need pruning too? We have things in our life that make us unhealthy or keep us from growing good spiritual fruit. God wants to prune those out.

How do you know if God is pruning you? Usually it means losing something that seems important but actually isn't. Maybe you've become a little too obsessed with a video game or social media. Or perhaps you're snacking on junk food all the time or reading books that give you bad dreams.

Just like those little suckers screaming, "Don't prune me! I'm impooooortant!" we don't want God to prune those things out of our lives. We think, "Video games are fun! Junk food makes me feel good! Books are good for me!"

But just like we need to prune those tomato suckers in order to get the biggest, best fruit, God needs to prune some unhealthy things out of our lives to help us grow the best fruit of the Spirit.

DISCUSSION STARTER

- Is God showing you something right now that he wants to prune in you? What is it?
- What would your life look like if you pruned video games, or junk food, or reading unhealthy books? How might you do it?

PRAYER

Thank you, God, for caring enough about us to prune away the things that don't bear good fruit. Please help us let you do this, even when we don't like it. Amen.

LOVE

HANDS-ON GROWTH ACTIVITIES

Use these activities as a hands-on supplement to the daily devotions. You can add in one per day, flip to this page for an idea only on days when you have a few extra minutes, or use a few of the activities each Sunday.

Memorize it: Memorize 1 John 4:19 or 1 John 4:16–19 together over the next two weeks.

Write it: Write a love letter to God.

Draw it: Draw a picture for God.

Pray it: Pray a breath prayer: As you breathe in, say, "You love me . . ." and as you breathe out, say, "and I love you."

Research it: How many times does the Bible talk about God's love?

Imagine it: Read 1 John 3:1. Do you know what "lavish" means? Let's imagine I'm lavishing icing on a cake. Should I put on just a tiny little bit? How about a medium-sized bit? How about a lot? When you lavish something, you are being extravagant and generous—you are giving a lot. This is how God loves you.

Play it: Make cookies and lavish on the icing in honor of God's lavish love for you!

Sing it: Make up a love song for God.

Ask it: What would be different if our God wasn't a loving God?

Speak it: Shout "I LOVE YOU" really loud!

For Bible verse printables and other activities,
please visit fruitofthespiritbook.com.

WHERE DOES LOVE COME FROM?

"I have loved you even as the Father has loved me.
Remain in my love."
(JOHN 15:9)

"For this is how God loved the world: He gave his one and only
Son, so that everyone who believes in him will not perish but
have eternal life."
(JOHN 3:16)

I want you to close your eyes for a moment. Imagine you have taken a time machine trip way back to the beginning of time. I mean the very beginning, before the universe existed. There are no hot dogs, no siblings, and no computers. Nothing to taste, smell, see, touch, or hear. All there is right here, right now, is God.

But here is the enormously strange mystery. While there is only one God, God exists as three persons. They are called Father, Spirit, and Son. The three persons of God are separate but the same, kind of like the three separate points on a fidget spinner. One fidget spinner has three points. But when you spin the fidget spinner, it all looks like one solid piece of plastic. God as three persons in one is called the Trinity.

These three persons love each other deeply. The Greek word for the relationship between Father, Spirit, and Son is *perichoresis* (pear-i-COR-i-sis). That's a very big word to describe something like a dance of love, where the Father, Son, and Spirit dance and swirl and rotate around a common center of divine love. They dance together in perfect love and peace.

Out of this love, God created you and me and everything around us, and God invites us to dance with him. In Genesis 1:26, God said, "Let us make human beings in our image, to be like us." We were designed to be part of this dance, to love God and love each other perfectly. But of course, we failed. God created laws to help us, but those laws only showed how unloving we were.

In John 15:9, Jesus said, "I have loved you even as the Father has loved me. Remain in my love." It's hard for us to remain in Jesus's love, isn't it? We have a hard time trusting that God actually loves us, which makes it hard to love him back.

So God, out of love, sent the Son to free us from our sin so we could join in this dance of love. All you have to do to join is accept that God has given you this gift, and choose to join the dance.

The Father created you, the Son saved you, and, once you accept the gift of salvation, the Holy Spirit lives inside you, helping you love God and love others.

DISCUSSION STARTER

- Where did Jesus's love come from?
- How do we become more loving? (Hint: It's not about trying harder or doing more.)

PRAYER

Father, Son, and Holy Spirit, thank you for loving each other and for loving us. Thank you for sending Jesus to us because of your great love for us. Jesus, please help us to remain in your love, just like you commanded. Amen.

DAY 12

MORE THAN A SPARROW

"What is the price of two sparrows—one copper coin? But not a
single sparrow can fall to the ground without your Father
knowing it. And the very hairs on your head are all numbered.
So don't be afraid; you are more valuable to God than
a whole flock of sparrows."
(MATTHEW 10:29–31)

Have you ever seen a sparrow? You probably have, but you may not remember it. Sparrows are small, brown, and boring. They're so boring and common, in fact, that people who track birds, called "birders," call them "Little Brown Jobs." They live everywhere and no one pays much attention to them.

Except God.

Even when they land on the ground and fly away, God notices them. Can you imagine noticing every single sparrow in the world land and take off again? I think we might go bonkers if we tried. But God can see them all.

Not only can God see all the sparrows going about their days, but he actually cares about them. He notices what they eat and when they lay eggs, when they go to sleep and when they're being chased by the neighborhood cat.

Jesus spoke these words to a group of people who had a very hard life. They were being bossed around by the Romans, and anyone who said something bad about the Romans was killed. They didn't have a lot of money, and some might have even been starving. The common people were small and unimportant. But Jesus told them that if God cares about the sparrows so much, he must care about people—his most special creation—even more.

So when you get up in the night with a stomachache, he cares. When you lose your special treasure, he cares. When you're being chased by the neighborhood cat, he cares. And when the really big stuff happens, he cares too.

God didn't say the sparrows wouldn't fall to the ground. He just said it wouldn't happen without him noticing and caring.

Bad things might happen to you too, but this doesn't mean that God has forgotten you or that he doesn't care. God cares about the boring, brown sparrows that are everywhere, and he cares about you even more. There is never a moment he stops caring for you. In fact, he cares about you so much that he knows exactly how many hairs are on your head.

You can trust God because he is absolutely, completely head-over-heels in love with you.

DISCUSSION STARTER

- Why do you think Jesus compared people to a boring bird instead of a fancy, beautiful bird?
- How many hairs do you think you have?
- Tell me about a time in your life when you thought God didn't care about you or someone else you know.

PRAYER

God, thank you that you care so very much for us. Please show us your love this week. Amen.

DAY 13

LOVING THE PRODIGAL

"So he returned home to his father. And while he was still a
long way off, his father saw him coming. Filled with love and
compassion, he ran to his son, embraced him, and kissed him."
(LUKE 15:20)

Have you ever disobeyed your mom or dad on purpose? Maybe you were
asked to get ready for bed, but you did something else instead. Or maybe
you were asked to set the table and you kept reading your book instead of
obeying.

When I was six years old, my friend asked me to come play on the hill by
the pond after school. When my mom asked why I was an hour late, I got
scared. Not only was I supposed to come straight home after school, but I
also wasn't supposed to be on the hill by the pond. I didn't want to get in
trouble, so I lied. Do you know how long it took me to tell my mom the truth
about that? Thirty years! Kind of ridiculous, isn't it?

The son in today's verse didn't just run away to play by the pond. He asked
for his dad's money so he could run away to a far-off land. Then he ran out
of money when there was a famine in the land, which meant there were
few jobs and not much food. He was starving to death. He remembered the
amazing food they ate at his father's house, and his empty stomach rumbled.
Could he go home? Would his father accept him as a servant, even though he
had been so awful?

There was only one way to find out. He trudged home, barefoot and
threadbare. He crafted the perfect apology in his mind. But while he was still
a long way off, his father spotted him.

When Jesus originally told this story, the listeners would have been really
shocked to hear what the father did. Instead of waiting calmly like a normal
Jewish dad, ready to give his son a lecture for his terrible choices, he rushed

out the door to hug his son. I can see him lifting his robes and dashing down the dusty path, jeweled sandals flipping up dust as he wept.

Did you know, we are just like the son in this story? You and I have walked away from God. We have both disobeyed and made bad choices and hurt other people. But when we turn back to him, we will always find he is like the father in this story: running toward us with arms open wide, tears of love pouring down his face.

DISCUSSION STARTER

- Tell about a time when you disobeyed. (Hey, parents, make sure you answer this one too!)
- Have you ever been forgiven when you expected to be punished? What did that forgiveness feel like?

PRAYER

Thank you, God, for giving us your incredibly deep love. May your lavish love soak deep into our hearts until we feel totally and completely secure. Amen.

DAY 14

LOVING THE PROUD

His father said to him, "Look, dear son, you have always stayed
by me, and everything I have is yours. We had to celebrate this
happy day. For your brother was dead and has come back to life!
He was lost, but now he is found!"
(LUKE 15:31–32)

Sometimes, it can be really hard to forgive. If someone has ever hurt your
feelings really deeply, you probably know what I mean. You might want to
forgive them, but every time you think of them, you just remember the mean
things they said about you.

Last time, we learned about a father with two sons. The younger brother
asked for his dad's money. When he got it, he ran away from home and
wasted it. Meanwhile, the older brother stayed at home, working in the fields
and obeying his dad. One day he came home from a hard day of work in the
fields. He was probably super sweaty and smelly, and to his surprise, there
was a party going on at his house. No one had told him about it, so he asked
what was going on. Imagine his surprise when he was told that his rude little
brother was home, and his dad had welcomed him back with a huge party!

The older brother was not impressed. In fact, he was so angry he wouldn't
even come inside the house. This was very disrespectful toward his father.
Again, the father did something normal Jewish dads would never do. You've
probably heard this story before, so it might not really surprise you. But the
people who first heard this story would have been shocked that he came out
of the house again and pleaded with his son to join in. Pleading was humili-
ating for any Jewish dad. But the father in this story didn't worry about what
other people thought of him. He just wanted his sons to be together in the
family. Did you notice what he said to this unforgiving son?

"You have always stayed by me, and everything I have is yours" (Luke

15:31). He showed the same kind of amazing forgiveness and love toward both sons. One was rebellious and the other was unforgiving and disrespectful, but he loved them both.

We've probably all behaved like the older brother in this story. You've seen a kid who was misbehaving and thought, "That's the bad kid." And if that kid hurt you or hurt your friend, you might not want to forgive him. But God wants us to show his love in the world, and that means forgiving people who have hurt us. Of course, it doesn't mean we necessarily let them back in our lives, but forgiveness is part of God's plan for us. Because God is an expert at forgiving his enemies, his Holy Spirit can change our hearts to help us forgive others.

DISCUSSION STARTER

- What is something God has forgiven you for?
- Who do you need to forgive?

PRAYER

Thank you, God, for your amazing gift of love and forgiveness. Please help us to know your deep love and share it with others. Amen.

DAY 15

THE DEEPEST LOVE

When Mary arrived and saw Jesus, she fell at his feet and
said, "Lord, if only you had been here, my brother
would not have died."
(JOHN 11:32)

Have you ever felt like your parents don't love you? Like, maybe your mom
makes you eat all your vegetables every single time, even when you're super
full. Or maybe you have lots of trouble with writing, and instead of helping
you, your dad makes you write even more. Sometimes, it seems like parents
let bad things happen to their kids. But loving parents only do it when they
know it's not actually a bad thing.

Sometimes we wonder the same thing about God. We ask, "Why would a
loving God let bad things happen?" It's easy to think love only shows up as
happy pink hearts that make us feel good, and if it doesn't make us feel good,
it's not love. But God's love is deeper than that, and sometimes things that
seem bad are actually good for us.

One day, Jesus heard that his good friend Lazarus was sick. Jesus had the
power to make Lazarus well again, but instead he chose to stay where he was
for two more days. When he finally got to Lazarus's home, his friend had been
dead four days. His sister Mary cried at Jesus's feet. She knew Jesus could have
healed Lazarus, but he had purposefully stayed away. It seemed like he was
just acting mean. Surely, if Jesus loved them, he would have come right away.

But Jesus did love them. He cried with Mary and Martha and reminded
them who he was. People whispered about him, wondering why he hadn't
come sooner. Suddenly, Jesus asked them to open the tomb. Martha said,
"Lord, he has been dead for four days. The smell will be terrible" (John 11:39).
Opening a four-day-old grave does not sound like my idea of a good time
(think about the stink!). But Jesus insisted.

They obeyed, and Jesus showed his amazing power and love by commanding Lazarus to come back to life. And he did! Lazarus walked out of the tomb, still wrapped in grave clothes. No, he wasn't a mummy. He was alive, living proof of Jesus's love.

Jesus let Lazarus die. He let Mary and Martha bury him and host a funeral. But when he brought Lazarus back to life, many new people began to believe in Jesus. He brought something amazing and beautiful out of something bad.

Sometimes Jesus lets bad things happen to us too. But he always brings something good out of it. It may not feel good all the time, but his love brings good out of bad and creates beauty from the ugly parts of life.

DISCUSSION STARTER

- Think of a time when something bad happened in your life (or in a movie, book, or Bible story). How did God made something good come from it?

PRAYER

Thank you, Jesus, that your love isn't just about making us feel good but about doing good in our lives. Help us to trust you when things are hard and to look for what you are doing in every situation. Amen.

DAY 16

LOVING GOD

Jesus replied, "You must love the LORD your God with all your
heart, all your soul, and all your mind." This is the first and
greatest commandment.
(MATTHEW 22:37–38)

It might seem strange that the God who created the sun and the planets and
all life on earth wants us to love him, but it's true! In fact, this is one of God's
two rules for life: love God with everything you've got.

What does it actually look like to show love to God? We can't exactly give
him a big hug or bake him a delicious cake, can we? We can learn what it
looks like to love God from Jesus and from some of the people of the Bible.

Jesus loved God by spending time in prayer and by doing the work God
the Father gave him to do: healing, preaching, and ultimately dying on the
cross. Jesus said in John 15:9, "I have loved you even as the Father has loved
me." Jesus's love came from the Father's love, which shows that we don't have
to fake our love for God. We just need to ask him for his love. When we experience his love for us, we want to love him back.

Loving God is easier to understand if we think about loving Jesus, who
was God in person, and could be touched and seen and smelled. So how did
the people around Jesus show love to him?

Mary and Joseph loved Jesus by being his parents. Shepherds loved Jesus
by telling everyone they met about the baby lying in the manger. The magi
loved Jesus by giving him gifts.

A different Mary loved Jesus by crying on his feet, wiping them with her
hair, and pouring perfume on him. Her sister, Martha, loved Jesus by prepar-
ing meals for him and his disciples.

Zacchaeus loved Jesus by giving away most of his money. Many of the
people Jesus healed loved him by being grateful. The disciples loved Jesus

by following and learning from him. Matthew, Mark, Luke, and John loved Jesus by writing down the details of his life on earth.

There are so many ways to love Jesus. But John wrote down what Jesus said about the best way to love him: "All who love me will do what I say. My Father will love them, and we will come and make our home with each of them. Anyone who doesn't love me will not obey me" (John 14:23–24).

One of the very best ways to love God is to study the Bible so we can learn what God wants, and then practice obeying him. That's exactly what we're doing right now! Look at you, loving God.

DISCUSSION STARTER

- Why do you think God wants to be loved?
- How can you show love to God today?

PRAYER

God, please make your home in us so we can experience your love and love you back by learning to obey you. Amen.

DAY 17

LOVING OTHERS

"A second is equally important:
'Love your neighbor as yourself.'"
(Matthew 22:39)

Hold up your arms and put them in the shape of a cross. One of your hands points vertically, straight up. The other hand points horizontally, to the side. Do you see where your fingers are pointing? This is a great reminder of the two commandments, or rules, that Jesus gave.

We learned the first rule last time: Love God with everything you've got. The vertical arm can help us remember God's love because it points up. (God is all around us, but we often think of him as being up.) We can love God because he first loved us and showed us his love through Jesus. The first step in following this command is to let God show you his very deep love for you. Sure, he loves the whole world, but he also loves you personally.

The other arm points sideways and reminds us of the other rule, which Jesus said is just as important: Love your neighbor as yourself. Sometimes this is the harder commandment to follow.

Have you ever had a hard time showing love to a sibling, to a mean kid at the park, or to an adult who isn't very nice to you? We've all had experiences with people who are hard to love. And yet, Jesus not only told us to love others as ourselves, but he even told us to love our enemies. Yikes! Now that's a hard one.

Jesus was able to show love to those who betrayed and arrested and killed him. He even showed love to the thieves on the crosses beside him, even though one of them mocked him.

Some days it might seem truly impossible to show love to your enemies or even to your brother. But guess what? With Jesus's power in you, you can love anyone. Here's the secret: it's actually not your love. It's God's love pouring out of you.

Let's go back to your arms pointing up and across. What would happen if someone poured juice down the middle of the cross? Would it stay nicely on your hand or would it splash out? Obviously, it would splash and make everything a sticky mess! (I don't recommend it.)

This is just like God's love. When you let it pour down on you, it naturally splashes out to other people.

When you know you're deeply loved, you don't live life out of fear, so you can be courageous and show love even to your enemies.

Are you ready? Set . . . love!

DISCUSSION STARTER

- Who do you find hard to love?
- What is one way you can show God's love to that person this week?

PRAYER

Jesus, you are so amazing. You loved your enemies, and you pour out your love on us. Thank you for filling us with your love so we can live in love and power too. Amen.

DAY 18

SPOTLESS LOVE

He took a cup of wine and gave thanks to God for it. He gave it
to them and said, "Each of you drink from it, for this is my blood,
which confirms the covenant between God and his people. It is
poured out as a sacrifice to forgive the sins of many."
(MATTHEW 26:27–28)

Have you ever planned a special surprise as a way to show your love for
someone? Maybe you planned a special gift for your mom or a special snack
to eat when your friend came over. God did the same thing. He planned a
very special event that would rescue the whole world, and he dropped clues
about it for thousands of years before it happened.

Over three thousand years ago, the Israelites were slaves in Egypt. God
planned to help them escape, but he wanted Pharaoh to admit God was more
powerful than the false gods the Egyptians worshipped. God sent ten plagues
to the people of Egypt, from frogs and bugs to skin sores and utter darkness.
Each plague proved God was more powerful than one of the Egyptian gods.
The tenth plague was the worst, and God gave Moses rules for how to escape
the plague. Each family was to kill and roast a lamb. It had to be perfect—no
spots allowed. When they killed the lamb, they were to take some of the
blood and paint it around their doors. The angel of death passed over every
house with blood-painted doorframes. The blood of the lamb saved them
from death. This was one of the first clues about God's rescue plan.

Every year, Jewish people celebrate their rescue from slavery in a festival
called the Passover. (It's a big deal, kind of like Christmas and Easter are
to us.) The Passover meal has more clues about God's rescue plan. The day
before he died, Jesus shared a Passover meal with his friends. You might have
heard this meal called "the Last Supper" because it was the last meal Jesus
had with his friends before he died.

Near the end of the Passover meal, Jesus picked up his cup of red wine and told his disciples it was his blood, and they should drink it. That sounds super gross, but Jesus didn't mean the wine was literally his blood. He was giving another clue about God's rescue plan. He meant that the red wine was to remind them of his blood. Normally, the red wine reminded the Israelites of the blood of the lamb. But just as the blood of the lamb saved the ancient Israelites, Jesus's blood (and death) would save anyone who believes in him.

Jesus's death wasn't an accident, and it didn't surprise him. In 1 Corinthians 5:7, one of Jesus's followers wrote, "Christ, our Passover Lamb, has been sacrificed for us." Jesus's death and resurrection was God's loving rescue plan. He planned it all out of his great love for us, to show us how amazing and powerful he is. And the best thing is, we get to be part of it by telling others about it!

DISCUSSION STARTER
- Tell about a time you planned a special surprise for someone.
- What is something special we could do this week to show God's love to someone? Let's plan it!

PRAYER
Thank you, Jesus, for loving us so much that you were willing to die for us. You are amazing. Help us to never forget your life-changing love. Amen.

DAY 19

PROVE IT TO THE WORLD

"Now I am giving you a new commandment: Love each other.
Just as I have loved you, you should love each other.
Your love for one another will prove to the world
that you are my disciples."
(JOHN 13:34–35)

Let's pretend we are private detectives. Pop on your detective hat, grab a notepad and a pen, and let's go people watching!

As private detectives, today we're trying to answer this question: How do you know if someone is a Christian? We might write in our notebooks, "Is kind to others. Doesn't swear or do drugs." Or maybe we would write, "Reads the Bible" or "Donates money to the church."

Those things might give us clues, but they don't actually tell us whether someone follows Jesus. Deep down, only God knows who is truly a Christian, but Jesus dropped a big clue during his Last Supper with his friends.

The night before he died, he had a special supper with them. He washed their feet and asked them to do the same for others, then hinted at his death. He was going to prove his amazing love for humans the very next day by dying for our sins. But before he did, Jesus gave this command to his disciples: Love each other.

Why did Jesus tell his disciples to love each other? It was a command, not a suggestion. Just as Jesus had showed love to them over and over again, they were to show love to each other over and over again.

But it was more than a command. It was proof. Their love for each other was supposed to be a huge, glaringly obvious clue to the world about who follows Jesus. We are supposed to prove to the world that we follow Jesus by being like him, by showing love to each other over and over.

We don't always do a great job. Christians fight about the color to paint the church, which instruments to play, how to spend our money, and who should be in charge of our country.

Even Christians within families yell at each other, hurt each other's feelings, and are generally just plain mean to each other sometimes (or a lot of times).

Loving each other is definitely not easy. But during the Last Supper, Jesus also promised the Holy Spirit, who helps us follow Jesus and obey the greatest commands: to love God and to love others. You can ask the Holy Spirit to help you obey Jesus by loving other Christians!

DISCUSSION STARTER

- If a private detective looked at our family, would they see clues that we are following Jesus? Which clues?
- Are there certain Christians you find it harder to love? Why is it hard for you to love them?

PRAYER

Jesus, we confess we don't always do a great job of loving each other. Please fill us to overflowing with your incredible love so we can show the world that following you can change lives. Amen.

DAY 20

RECONCILING LOVE

The crowd watched and the leaders scoffed. "He saved others,"
they said, "let him save himself if he is really God's Messiah,
the Chosen One."
(LUKE 23:35)

If you were dying in a hospital and had the power to save yourself by just
getting out of your hospital bed, would you do it? I sure would!

The Bible tells us when Jesus was on the cross, the crowd laughed at Jesus
and said, "If you are the King of the Jews, save yourself!" (Luke 23:37). They
assumed if Jesus really was God's Son and had the power of God, he would
want to save himself and have the power to save himself.

He didn't get off the cross, though. So either he *didn't want* to save himself,
or he *wasn't able* to save himself.

Jesus really *is* God's Son, and he could have disintegrated the cross with
a thought or blasted his enemies into the Dead Sea. It wasn't the nails in his
hands and feet keeping Jesus on the cross. It wasn't the Pharisees or Romans
or anyone else who kept Jesus on the cross. It wasn't even the soldiers with
their deadly spears who kept Jesus on the cross. If he had wanted to come
down, he could have, nails and all.

Instead, it was *love* that kept Jesus on the cross.

Colossians 1:19–20 says:

> For God in all his fullness
>   was pleased to live in Christ,
> and through him God reconciled
>   everything to himself.
> He made peace with everything in heaven and on earth
>   by means of Christ's blood on the cross.

Reconcile means "to make something right." Jesus knew his death would make the relationship between God and his people right again.

Jesus didn't want to save himself because he knew his death would save you and me. Getting off the cross would have been selfish and unloving, which is exactly the opposite of who Jesus is.

After being on the cross for hours, Jesus said, "It is finished!" (John 19:30). His great love for us had done what nothing else could ever do: reconcile us to God. He bowed his head and let himself die because he had done the hardest but most amazing thing in the whole world. He laid down his life for his friends . . . and his enemies.

As Jesus's follower, Jesus calls you to join in the work of reconciling. No, he doesn't want you to die on a cross! But you get to join him in making the world right again by showing his love every day. Isn't that an amazing job?

DISCUSSION STARTER

- What will you say to Jesus in response to his incredible love for you?
- What is one problem in the world that bothers you? Ask Jesus to give you courage and ideas to help you join the work of making it right.

PRAYER

Jesus, you are so good to us. Thank you for laying down your life for us, and for making peace through your blood, shed on the cross. Thank you that we get to be part of bringing your love to the world. Give us courage to do this each day. Amen.

JOY

HANDS-ON GROWTH ACTIVITIES

Use these activities as a hands-on supplement to the daily devotions. You can add in one per day, flip to this page for an idea only on days when you have a few extra minutes, or use a few of the activities each Sunday.

Memorize it: Memorize Psalm 126:2 together over the next two weeks.

Write it: Write out Psalm 126:2 in bubble letters and hang it on your wall.

Draw it: Draw a joyful picture for God.

Pray it: Pray a breath prayer: As you breathe in, say, "You bring me joy . . ." and as you breathe out, say, "and I bring you joy."

Research it: What does the Bible say about humor and laughter?

Imagine it: Close your eyes and think about things that make you feel happy. How many can you think of? Feel that feeling? That is just a tiny part of what joy really is.

Play it: Make a sculpture of one of the JOY Bible stories. (Use blocks, dough, popsicle sticks, or whatever you have on hand.)

Sing it: Make up a song of joy for God.

Ask it: What would be different if our God wasn't a joyful God?

Speak it: Play the "ha" game with at least one other person. The first person says "ha," the second person says "haha," and you keeping adding one ha after another until you are all giggling!

For Bible verse printables and other activities,
please visit fruitofthespiritbook.com.

DAY 21

JOY-FILLED OBEDIENCE

"I have loved you even as the Father has loved me. Remain in
my love. When you obey my commandments, you remain in my
love, just as I obey my Father's commandments and remain in his
love. I have told you these things so that you will be filled with
my joy. Yes, your joy will overflow!"
(JOHN 15:9–11)

The last ten devotions were all about love, and we're moving on to joy now.
But did you know that love and joy are connected? When we love, we'll find
joy too. Here's why.

Most people think certain types of dogs are naturally more aggressive
than others. But actually, an aggressive dog is more likely to be caused by a
certain type of dog *owner* than by a certain type of dog.

A dog owned by a master who punishes him by hitting or kicking him is
much more likely to hurt humans. He'll be more aggressive to strangers and
family. He won't obey, he won't be kind, and he won't be sweet. This is because
a dog that is punished a lot will feel anxious and stressed. Punishment can
also make your dog act even crazier instead of calming him down.

However, a dog trained by a loving master who rewards him for good
behavior, feeds him regularly, and gives him lots of ear scratches is more
likely to be calm and well-behaved. A dog that is well-loved is usually
well-behaved because he will respond well to correction.

What kind of puppy would you rather come home to: one that growls at
you because he's afraid of you or one that runs to the door, ears flapping and
panting happily? Personally, I'd pick the dog that was full of love because his
love and obedience bring me joy.

That's exactly what Jesus is talking about in this passage. Just like your
puppy will listen and obey with a joyful heart when you treat him with love,

you and I will be able to obey God with joyful hearts when we know God's love for us.

Sometimes adults make being a Christian sound like it's all about plain old obedience. That can make us want to rebel against God. We don't want someone else to be our master!

But when we truly love God like a puppy loves his good master, we trust God to be our master and willingly obey him. This brings the joy we so desperately want, and *that's* how love and joy are connected.

DISCUSSION STARTER

- Is there someone you find hard to obey? Why?
- Do you normally think of Jesus as being joyful? What scene can you think of where Jesus might have laughed or smiled or showed joy?

PRAYER

Jesus, thank you for showing us what it looks like to love and obey God with a happy heart. Help us to grow in joy as we grow in obedience. Amen.

DAY 22

LIFE OF THE PARTY

Later, Matthew invited Jesus and his disciples to his home as
dinner guests, along with many tax collectors and other
disreputable sinners. . . .
One day the disciples of John the Baptist came to Jesus and asked
him, "Why don't your disciples fast like we do and
the Pharisees do?"
Jesus replied, "Do wedding guests mourn while celebrating with
the groom? Of course not. But someday the groom will be taken
away from them, and then they will fast."
(MATTHEW 9:10, 14–15)

This passage doesn't really sound like it's about joy, but it is. The problem is
that only part of the story is written down, so we have to fill in the blanks a bit.

The religious leaders thought being good meant fasting, which means giving up food (or something else that's important to you). You might give up
eating junk food or a TV show for a while in order to help you get closer to
God. Fasting is normally a fairly serious thing. Part of the reason the religious leaders didn't like Jesus was that he was always going to parties! That's
basically the opposite of fasting. The leaders didn't think Jesus was serious
enough, which is funny, because nowadays we often think Jesus is very serious (and maybe a little bit boring).

Here's where we need to use our God-given imaginations a bit, because the
Bible doesn't really tell us about Jesus's personality. We don't know exactly
what Jesus did at those parties, but Jesus is God's Son, and God invented
laughter and joy and celebration. Did Jesus sit in the corner and teach? Did
he dance? Did he laugh? Did he ever make funny faces? I think he did all of
those things. Jesus must have been a lot of fun at parties, or people wouldn't
have kept inviting him. Party poopers don't get many invitations.

Jesus compared his time with his disciples to being part of a wedding. No one fasts at a wedding. They sing and dance and make jokes.

Here's one more thing about parties: it's hard to have a party if you're by yourself. That would be a very sad party, don't you think? The joy of a party is about being with friends. It's about playing games and laughing and eating together.

We often experience deeper joy when we're with others. It's great to sit in the corner and read the Bible, but the deepest joy is about being together with Jesus and those we love.

DISCUSSION STARTER

- Why do you think Jesus celebrated so often?
- Is this the image you had in your mind of Jesus? Why or why not?
- At what times do you feel the most joyful?

PRAYER

God, please show us what true joy looks like. Help us experience your deep joy together, no matter what happens this week. Amen.

DAY 23

CREATOR OF JOY

"A host always serves the best wine first," he said. "Then, when everyone has had a lot to drink, he brings out the less expensive wine. But you have kept the best until now!"
(JOHN 2:10)

Have you ever been to a wedding? Here's what normally happens: the bride and groom promise to love each other forever, the pastor pronounces them married, then there's a lot of smooching. After that, the married couple throws a party. This is not any old party either. It's a feast. There is a ton of fancy food and the biggest cake you've ever seen (and more smooching too). At the very end, there's usually a dance where everyone laughs and goes happy-crazy.

Once, Jesus and his friends were invited to a wedding. During the celebration, something horrible happened: they ran out of wine. This may not seem like a big deal to you, but the wine was a very special part of the wedding. Having a wedding party that ran out of wine would be like getting to the end of a birthday party and realizing someone forgot to bring the birthday cake.

Jesus's mom pulled him aside and said, "They have no more wine." I can imagine Jesus shaking his head as he said, "Dear woman, that's not our problem. . . . My time has not yet come." Even so, his mom turned to the servants and told them to obey him. (Isn't it funny that she kind of ignored his reason? I guess moms really do know best—even when their son is the Son of God!)

Jesus asked them to fill six huge stone jars with water. These jars were important. When Jewish people came home from work or went to the temple, they had to wash. The rules said a person had to be clean before they could be with God. But Jesus took the water from those jars and turned it into something joyful: the best wine the partiers ever had.

By using those jars, he was saying something special about his purpose.

Jesus came because God doesn't just want us to follow rules. Following rules is important and helpful. But because we can never follow the rules perfectly, Jesus came to show us a better way. The better way is an actual friendship with Jesus, where we accept his love and forgiveness. When we have a true friendship with Jesus, there is joy.

Jesus turning that water into wine would be like him taking a loaf of perfectly sliced bread and turning it into a fully frosted birthday cake with all the best toppings. And then I imagine he would turn on some music and get a dance party going. Doesn't he sound like an amazing, joy-filled friend?

DISCUSSION STARTER

- Tell about a time you felt joyful.
- What are some of the reasons you follow Jesus?

PRAYER

Thank you, Jesus, for making a way for us to have a relationship with you. Please fill us with more of your joy today, and help us to bring your joy to others. Amen.

DAY 24

THE TREASURE

"The Kingdom of Heaven is like a treasure that a man
discovered hidden in a field. In his excitement, he hid it again
and sold everything he owned to get enough money to buy
the field. Again, the Kingdom of Heaven is like a merchant on
the lookout for choice pearls. When he discovered a pearl of
great value, he sold everything he owned and bought it!"
(MATTHEW 13:44–46)

Have you ever gone on a treasure hunt? I think it would be marvelous!

Imagine you find a map with a big red X on it. Your heart beats a little faster. *Could it be true that you really found a treasure map? What could the treasure be?* You don't want to tell anyone at first, because what if they got to the treasure before you and took it? That would be more disappointing than missing Christmas. But you have to make some plans. How will you get there? What will you bring?

At last, you gather what you need. The map brings you to a nearby park, the one with big trees, some grass, and even a sandbox. How is it possible that no one has found the treasure yet? You bite your lip, hoping it's still there, then glance around to make sure no one is watching. You slip behind the biggest tree at the edge of the park. The map is unfurled for one final look to make sure you're digging in the right spot. Taking an enormous breath, you ram your shovel into the dirt near the base of the tree. Again and again you pull up shovelfuls of plain dirt. Sweat trickles down your face.

And then, your shovel hits something hard. Trembling, you reach down to brush off the dirt. It's a box! After freeing the box from the ground, you brush off your filthy hands on your shirt; you don't want to get the treasure dirty. After a quick peek around the tree to make sure no one has noticed, you crack open the box. Something inside gleams.

Wow, isn't finding treasure exciting? I think that's why Jesus used the image of finding a treasure as one way to describe the Kingdom of Heaven. The Kingdom of Heaven isn't just about going to heaven when you die. It's about knowing God's here and following him here on earth too. Sometimes we only think of the hard parts of the Kingdom of Heaven—choosing unselfishness, loving our enemies, and giving to others. But Jesus wanted us to know that the Kingdom of Heaven is an amazing treasure! It can make us just as joyful as finding a crown or a pile of jewels in the park.

DISCUSSION STARTER

- What is something exciting you have experienced because of Jesus?
- What do you think is the difference between joy and happiness?

PRAYER

Thank you, Jesus, for the incredible joy we find in your kingdom. Even on the days when we don't feel happy, help us to feel the deep joy of being part of your kingdom. And may we bring your joy to everyone around us! Amen.

DAY 25

JOYFUL RETURN

"If a man has a hundred sheep and one of them gets lost,
what will he do? Won't he leave the ninety-nine others in the
wilderness and go to search for the one that is lost until he finds
it? And when he has found it, he will joyfully carry it home on
his shoulders. When he arrives, he will call together his friends
and neighbors, saying, 'Rejoice with me because I have
found my lost sheep.'"
(LUKE 15:4–6)

Here's how a shepherd cares for a flock of sheep. First, the sheep need food
and water. But the shepherd doesn't bring the food and water *to* the sheep,
like you might bring slop to a pigpen or put dog food in a dish. Instead, the
shepherd must bring the flock out to the fields each day, helping them find
fresh grass to eat. While out there, the sheep are vulnerable to predators—big
animals that think a lamb is a juicy dinner. The shepherd also has to defend
the sheep. But sheep are also a little silly. A sheep will see a juicy bit of grass
just a little farther away and trot off to taste it. It doesn't take long before a
sheep can disappear behind a bush and be easy prey for a wolf.

In Jesus's story, the shepherd has a hundred sheep! This isn't some poor fel-
low with just one or two sheep. If one gets lost, he still has ninety-nine sheep.
That's a lot of sheep names to remember! He could just shrug his shoulders
and not worry about the one missing sheep. But in Jesus's story, the shepherd
leaves the ninety-nine. (But wait. The Bible doesn't say the other sheep were
left in a sheep pen. They were left in the wilderness! Doesn't that seem a little
foolish? Often, the things that God does seem foolish to us because we don't
understand his plans.)

The shepherd in this story goes to search for the one sheep that got lost,
and then he joyfully carries it home on his shoulders. There's so much joy; he

is joyful when he first finds the sheep and when he's lugging it home, and he also rejoices with his friends and neighbors. All over one silly sheep.

That's just how Jesus feels about us. He told this story because the religious leaders criticized him for hanging out with people who had made bad choices. He wanted to show that it brings God joy when any person comes to him and says, "I'm sorry," no matter how many bad things they have done. Whether you get in trouble every single day, or you only make mistakes once per week, Jesus is so excited when you truly apologize to him. No one is too bad, too mean, or too naughty for Jesus to love.

DISCUSSION STARTER

- What are some things you got in trouble for this week?
- Spend some time apologizing to Jesus. (Parents, you too!)

PRAYER

Jesus, we are all like that lost sheep. We wander away from you and forget the joy that comes from living with you. Thank you for bringing us back to you and rejoicing over us! Amen.

DAY 26

JOYFUL DISCOVERY

"Suppose a woman has ten silver coins and loses one. Won't she
light a lamp and sweep the entire house and search carefully
until she finds it? And when she finds it, she will call in her
friends and neighbors and say, 'Rejoice with me because I have
found my lost coin.'"
(LUKE 15:8–9)

Have you ever lost some money? It's so easy for a coin to fall out of your pocket and roll away. But today's story isn't about someone who just lost a few small coins under a vending machine. She lost part of her life savings.

Most men earned just one silver coin each day and that was just enough to feed the family. They were not rich people, and it would have been very hard to save money. Most of the money they did have was taken as taxes by the Romans, which means a woman with ten silver coins wasn't a rich woman. Instead, she was probably someone who knew how to save a bit of money so her family wouldn't starve when her husband had to take a sick day.

Then one day, perhaps as she was making sure her coins were still in the jar, one slipped out of her fingers and onto the floor. She would have had either a dirt floor covered in straw or a floor made from stones, with lots of cracks in between. Either would have had lots of hiding places for a tiny coin. To make things harder, people in those days didn't have big windows or electricity. Their homes were dark.

So this woman lit a lamp, pulled out her broom, and began to search for her lost coin. *Whisk, whisk, whisk* went the broom as she listened for a tinkle of the coin. She lowered the lamp into every corner, praying that she would find the precious coin. Then, there it was! She snatched it off the ground before it could roll away again and held it close to her heart. She called her friends and neighbors to come and rejoice with her because her lost coin had been found.

Jesus told this story to teach us something new about God: that he cares about each of us. He doesn't just care about the whole world; he cares about *you*. Even today, most people imagine God as an angry old man who strikes people down with lightning bolts. But that's not our God. Our God is a loving God who actively seeks you, even if you want to hide.

When might you want to hide from God? Well, imagine you had a big fight with a friend, and it was all your fault. Your friend isn't talking to you and you don't know how to fix it and you don't want to talk to God about it because you'll have to admit you did something wrong. But God cares so much about you that he doesn't want to leave you sitting in misery. He will remind you of what you did wrong, not so you can feel guilty but so you can apologize. That reminder is what it feels like when God seeks you. When you apologize to God, he forgives you and helps you rebuild your friendship. That's what it's like to be found by God! When you let him find you, he rejoices!

DISCUSSION STARTER

- Tell about a time you did something wrong and you felt bad about it until you apologized. How did you feel after apologizing?

PRAYER

Thank you, God, for looking for us and for reminding us to apologize. Thank you that you take joy in helping us live better lives with you. Amen.

DAY 27

GOD'S REASON FOR JOY

"His father said to the servants, 'Quick! Bring the finest robe in
the house and put it on him. Get a ring for his finger and sandals
for his feet. And kill the calf we have been fattening. We must
celebrate with a feast, for this son of mine was dead and has now
returned to life. He was lost, but now he is found.'
So the party began."
(LUKE 15:22–24)

Jesus told three stories about lost things: a lost sheep, a lost coin, and a lost
son. In the stories, each one is lost for a different reason.

In the first story, the sheep wanders away because it is foolish. In the next
story, the coin just rolls away and gets lots. In the story of the prodigal son,
the son takes his dad's money and runs away.

We are like all of those things, at some point in our lives.

Sometimes we're just foolish, like that sheep. We make a dumb choice and
it gets us into trouble. Maybe you choose to hang out with a friend who is
lots of fun but steals little things from other kids. After a while, you forget it's
wrong to steal, so you join in.

Sometimes we forget about God and roll away, like the coin. Our daily
lives get busy with sports and schoolwork and friends and we forget God
wants to spend time with us.

Other times, we choose to sin and run away from God, like the prodigal
son. You might choose to be mean to an annoying kid instead of showing
love.

In each of Jesus's stories, someone goes on a rescue mission: a shepherd,
a woman, and a father running from his house. That character represents
God, rescuing people who are lost and need his love. He looks for us whether
we're foolish, forgetful, or disobedient.

But I think the best part of each story is that the rescuer rejoices when their rescue mission is successful. In the story of the prodigal son, the dad even throws a huge party. This reminds us that God doesn't come rescue us so he can lecture us. He wants us back because it brings him joy.

God loves us so deeply, and he knows that when we understand his love, our hearts and lives will change, and we'll *want* to love our enemies, spend time with him, and choose kindness. This brings him deep joy, and it overflows into our hearts, bringing us joy as well. What could be better than joining God on the rescue mission?

DISCUSSION STARTER

- If God threw a party for you, what would it look like?
- How can our family join God on his rescue mission?

PRAYER

Thank you, God, that you rejoice over us when we turn back to you. May your joy spill over into our hearts so we can be part of your great rescue mission. Amen.

DAY 28

JOY IN SADNESS

Then they sang a hymn and went out to the Mount of Olives.
(MATTHEW 26:30)

Have you ever had a feeling that something was about to go horribly wrong? Maybe your mom just dropped you off for the day and you realized you forgot your lunch. Or you were running fast and stumbled, getting that feeling just as you were about to face-plant.

The night before he died, Jesus knew it was going to happen. He knew many of his friends would betray him or run away. He knew he would be put on trial. And he knew he would die.

Yet as he walked away from his last meal with his friends, they sang a song together. That seems like an odd thing to do when you have so much on your mind, but when you know exactly what he was singing, it's even more mind-boggling.

We know exactly what Jesus was singing because he had just celebrated the Passover with his friends. Jewish people always sing Psalms 113–118 during Passover, saving a few of the psalms for after the party is over.

Let's take a look at a few parts of Psalm 118.

Jesus sang:

> The LORD is for me, so I will have no fear.
> What can mere people do to me?
> Yes, the LORD is for me; he will help me.
> I will look in triumph at those who hate me. (vv. 6–7)

Jesus knew he could trust his Father to help him. He didn't need to be afraid of his enemies. And even though Jesus knew he was about to die, he also knew why he was dying, and he was able to rejoice:

The LORD is my strength and my song;
he has given me victory. (v. 14)

Jesus was singing of joy and victory on the worst night of his life. Wow.

That reminds me of something Jesus's brother wrote many years later: "When troubles of any kind come your way, consider it an opportunity for great joy" (James 1:2).

James didn't mean that you have to paste a smile on your face and pretend to be happy. It's OK to be sad. But Jesus shows us that with the Holy Spirit, it is possible to find times of joy even when bad things happen. The best way to feel that joy is to notice things you can be grateful for. When you're sad, does your puppy gives you snuggles? Or do you climb a tree to the highest branch and watch the clouds? Those are the kinds of moments we can thank God for, even when life is hard.

DISCUSSION STARTER

- Tell about a time something bad happened. Was there anything during that bad time that made you smile?

PRAYER

Thank you, Jesus, for showing what joy looks like, even when life is hard. Please remind us to praise you in the midst of every situation so we can learn to live with joy too. Amen.

DAY 29

JOY IN THE MORNING

"I tell you the truth, you will weep and mourn over what is
going to happen to me, but the world will rejoice. You will grieve,
but your grief will suddenly turn to wonderful joy."
(JOHN 16:20)

After Jesus died on the cross, his friends were heartbroken. They thought he was going to be the king and save them from the Romans. All their plans and hopes were now destroyed, like beads from a broken necklace, bouncing and rolling under every cupboard and bed.

They were sad to lose their friend, disappointed that he hadn't saved them, angry at those who killed him, and scared they'd be crucified too. That's a lot of feelings. Have you ever felt like crying and screaming and hiding under the bed, all at the same time?

Jesus had predicted this sad time when he said, "You will weep and mourn over what is going to happen to me, but the world will rejoice" (John 16:20). In fact, Jesus's friends were terrified, so they did a lot of hiding in locked rooms. (I wonder if any of them hid under the bed too?)

Guess who wasn't quite so scared? The women. The Sunday after his death, Jesus's mom and her friends went to Jesus's tomb. They planned to rub funeral spices on his body, but they got a big shock when they got there! The earth rumbled and shook. They might have wondered if a platoon of soldiers was coming to arrest and crucify them too. But instead, the nearby soldiers fainted in terror. The rumble wasn't from marching soldiers. It was from an angel rolling back the ginormous rock covering the door of Jesus's tomb.

The women must have looked terrified because the angel said to them, "'Don't be afraid! . . . I know you are looking for Jesus, who was crucified. He isn't here! He is risen from the dead, just as he said would happen'" (Matthew 28:5–6).

Jesus was always giving them clues about his death and resurrection, but still, what a surprise! Jesus had promised, "You will grieve, but your grief will suddenly turn to wonderful joy" (John 16:20). Now that part of the prophecy was coming true! The Bible says the women were frightened but also full of intense joy as they rushed to give the angel's message to the men.

Did you know you can be joyful and scared at the same time? Joy is a gift from God that moves into your heart, and it stays there no matter what other feelings you have. The next time you're feeling scared in the night or worried about someone, ask God to help you feel his joy too.

DISCUSSION STARTER

- Can you think of a time (in real life or in a movie or book) when something awful happened, but then something amazing and joyful came out of it?

PRAYER

Thank you, Jesus, for bringing amazing, surprising joy. Please help us keep growing in your joy, no matter what happens in our lives. Amen.

DAY 30

BURSTING WITH JOY

Mary Magdalene found the disciples and told them,
"I have seen the Lord!"
(JOHN 20:18)

Have you ever given a presentation? Maybe you read a report out loud in front of your class, or you played piano in a recital, or you explained a game to a group of kids. It can be nerve-racking to speak (or play piano!) in front of a group of people. You might have been afraid you'd mess up, or they'd laugh at you or wouldn't understand you.

Mary Magdalene had that problem too. She was the very first person to see Jesus after he was resurrected. After the angel told her and her friends that Jesus was alive, she turned to leave the tomb.

A mysterious man stood there, whom she assumed was the gardener.

"'Dear woman, why are you crying?' [the man] asked her. 'Who are you looking for?'" (John 20:15).

Mary had all her sorrow and fear and confusion tangled up inside her like a knotted mess of string, and she couldn't even look at him.

"'Sir,' she said, 'if you have taken him away, tell me where you have put him, and I will go and get him'" (v. 15).

Even though the angels had said Jesus was alive, she couldn't quite believe it. Her tangled feelings kept her from seeing who this man really was. But Jesus didn't leave her in her mess.

He called her name, "Mary!" Finally, she turned. There, standing in front of her, whole and healthy and smiling at her, was Jesus. He really was alive!

Mary would have liked nothing better than to stay right where she was, clinging to Jesus and full of joy. But he didn't let her. Instead, he gave her a message to share. He said, "Go find my brothers and tell them, 'I am ascending to my Father and your Father, to my God and your God'" (v. 17).

In ancient Israel, women weren't considered good witnesses. Many men thought you couldn't trust a woman's story because she might change it, or she might lie. But Jesus chose Mary, a woman, to be the first person to see him alive. Both Peter and John had also been at the tomb, but Jesus didn't appear to them first. It was no accident; Jesus chose her.

And you know what? Even though people might not believe her, Mary busted out of that garden with enough joy and courage to tell anyone and everyone about Jesus! Our joy in Jesus isn't meant to be kept in our hearts and thought about on Sundays. He wants us to share it with our world . . . even if it's sometimes a little uncomfortable.

DISCUSSION STARTER

- When is a time you felt joyful because of Jesus?
- How can we, as a family, share God's joy with others?

PRAYER

Jesus, please take the truths we have learned and plant them deep in our hearts so they grow the fruit of joy in our lives. Give us courage to share your joy with others. Amen.

PEACE

HANDS-ON GROWTH ACTIVITIES

Use these activities as a hands-on supplement to the daily devotions. You can add in one per day, flip to this page for an idea only on days when you have a few extra minutes, or use a few of the activities each Sunday.

Memorize it: Memorize John 14:27 together over the next two weeks.

Write it: Write John 14:27 in fancy letters. Hang it on your wall.

Draw it: Draw a picture of yourself and Jesus being peaceful in the middle of a storm.

Pray it: Pray a breath prayer: As you breathe in, say, "When I am afraid . . ." and as you breathe out, say, "I will trust in you."

Research it: Can you find other storms in the Bible where God kept people safe?

Imagine it: Close your eyes and imagine being in a lake in the middle of a huge storm. Thunder crashes and waves slosh water up your nose. You can't touch the bottom no matter how far you stretch your toes. Now imagine Jesus next to you. As he holds you, an unpoppable bubble forms around you both. How does it feel to be protected?

Play it: Find some bubble solution (or make your own). Blow the biggest, best bubbles you can, and then pop them. Remember that God can help us find peace no matter what is happening in our lives.

Sing it: Find (or make up) a song about God's peace.

Ask it: What would be different if our God wasn't a peaceful God?

Speak it: Say John 14:27 in different voices. Try it loud, whispered, or wiggling your lips with your finger to make it sound bubbly.

For Bible verse printables and other activities,
please visit fruitofthespiritbook.com.

DAY 31

PRINCE OF PEACE

For a child is born to us,
a son is given to us.
The government will rest on his shoulders.
And he will be called:
Wonderful Counselor, Mighty God,
Everlasting Father, Prince of Peace.
(ISAIAH 9:6)

Seven hundred years before Jesus was born, the people of Jerusalem were terrified. Enemies attacked them from all sides. Even people who used to be their friends were trying to take over the city. The people of Jerusalem didn't know who was a friend and who was an enemy. They desperately needed peace.

In the middle of this scary time, God gave Isaiah a prophecy about a child who would be the Wonderful Counselor, Mighty God, Everlasting Father, and the Prince of Peace. Can you imagine signing your name on schoolwork if you had that many names? For today, let's zoom in on one name: Prince of Peace.

When you think of a prince, what comes to mind? Maybe you think of a fairy-tale prince who saves the day by kissing princesses and singing with squirrels. Or maybe it's a real-life prince who comes to mind, trotting through town, blowing kisses to the ladies on the way to a crucial battle.

In ancient times, a prince was often in charge of his father's army. His job was to bring war, not peace. Clearly, Jesus is a very different kind of prince. He brings peace instead of war.

In fact, Jesus is the prince of three different kinds of peace.

1. Jesus came to bring peace between us and God. Because of our sin, we were enemies of God. But Jesus made peace through his death and resurrection. Colossians 1:20 says,

Through him God reconciled
everything to himself.
He made peace with everything in heaven and on earth
by means of Christ's blood on the cross.

2. Jesus came to bring peace between people. Have you ever been in a
    fight? Yeah, me too. Jesus came to help us love our neighbors as our-
    selves. Ephesians 2:14 says, "Christ himself has brought peace to us.
    He united Jews and Gentiles into one people when, in his own body
    on the cross, he broke down the wall of hostility that separated us."
3. Jesus came to bring peace to our hearts. All those times we are afraid
    of the dark, afraid of other people, afraid of looking silly—Jesus came
    to free us from that! In John 14:27, Jesus says, "I am leaving you with
    a gift—peace of mind and heart. And the peace I give is a gift the
    world cannot give. So don't be troubled or afraid."

DISCUSSION STARTER

- What kind of peace would you like more of today?
- How could we point other people to the Prince of Peace?

PRAYER

Thank you, Jesus, for being the Prince of Peace. Please help us to trust you
more and live in peace with you, with others, and in our hearts. Amen.

DAY 32

PEACE IN THE STORM

Jesus got into the boat and started across the lake with his disciples. Suddenly, a fierce storm struck the lake, with waves breaking into the boat. But Jesus was sleeping. The disciples went and woke him up, shouting, "Lord, save us! We're going to drown!" Jesus responded, "Why are you afraid? You have so little faith!" Then he got up and rebuked the wind and waves, and suddenly there was a great calm. The disciples were amazed. "Who is this man?" they asked. "Even the winds and waves obey him!"
(MATTHEW 8:23–27)

Have you ever experienced a huge, ferocious storm? Maybe you live in an area that has tornadoes or hurricanes, but even a noisy thunderstorm can be scary enough to make me quiver under my blanket.

In this story, the disciples didn't expect to be stuck in a storm. It blew up when they were in the middle of the lake. There was nothing they could do except dump water out of the boat and pray. And what was Jesus doing this whole time? Sleeping! He must have had some serious earplugs to have been able to sleep through that.

We don't usually expect to be caught in storms either. I don't mean actual storms, like with wind and rain and lightning. I mean the kind of storm where everything in your life suddenly seems to go wrong.

Maybe you used to be really good at something and suddenly it feels like you're bad at it, or a friend decides they don't like you anymore, or your parents seem to get mad at you all the time.

Sometimes the storms of life can be even bigger. Maybe you've moved, your parents divorced, or someone died. All of it is surprising. It can seem like God is sleeping on the job, just like Jesus was sleeping in that boat.

But the good news is that God is never asleep on the job. Psalm 121:3 tells us that "the one who watches over you will not slumber."

God is always in charge, even when it looks like he's sleeping or like he's not listening. Our great God listens, and cares, and we can have peace in the storms of life.

DISCUSSION STARTER

- Why were the disciples afraid when Jesus wasn't? Do you think there are times in your life when you're afraid but Jesus is not? Why isn't Jesus afraid?
- Have you ever felt like God wasn't listening to your prayers?

PRAYER

Jesus, sometimes it feels like you're still asleep, not listening to our prayers. But thank you that you always listen to us and care about us. Help us to trust you and to have peace in the storms of life. Amen.

DAY 33

PRAYERFUL PEACE

Immediately after this, Jesus insisted that his disciples get back
into the boat and cross to the other side of the lake, while he sent
the people home. After sending them home, he went up into the
hills by himself to pray. Night fell while he was there alone.
Meanwhile, the disciples were in trouble far away from land,
for a strong wind had risen, and they were fighting heavy
waves. About three o'clock in the morning Jesus came toward
them, walking on the water.
(MATTHEW 14:22–25)

Wait, didn't we just read about the disciples getting caught in a storm? And
now they're in another one? Wow. Remind me never to get in a boat with
them. (On the other hand, they did get to experience some rather phenom-
enal things during those storms, so maybe I should be willing to sail with
them.)

While they were in this particular storm, Jesus was praying. Want to know
why he was praying? That very day he had heard that his cousin John had
been beheaded. Yikes. He took his disciples to a quiet place to pray and probably deal with his grief, but the crowds chased him. He healed them and fed
them (over five thousand of them!), then sent the disciples across the lake and
the crowds back home. What a busy day! Jesus got awful news, was chased
by crowds, then worked all day. He needed a break. So he prayed.

I don't know about you, but when I'm feeling horrible, I sometimes forget
that God can bring me peace. Prayer isn't always the first thing I think of.
Instead, I might have a nap or a bath or just stare at the wall for a while. Then
when those things don't bring me peace, I finally remember to pray!

These verses tell us that Jesus prayed from the time he sent the crowds
home until three o'clock in the morning. That's a lot of prayer! Then he did

something that was a miracle: he walked on water. Do you think his prayers helped him walk on top of the lake in the middle of a storm? I think so. He was so connected to the Father that he felt at complete peace and was able to carry that peace around like a bubble so the waves didn't affect him at all.

Jesus can help us live with that kind of peace too. We might not be able to walk on water, but Jesus can help us stay peaceful through hard times. We just need to *remember* to talk to him and to let him share his peace with us.

DISCUSSION STARTER

- When life is hard, what other things do you normally do before you remember to pray?
- What's one way that we can remind each other to pray first?

PRAYER

Jesus, teach us how to pray! Remind us to turn to you first instead of last. Help us find our peace in you. Amen.

DAY 34

PERFECT PEACE

When the disciples saw him walking on the water, they were
terrified. In their fear, they cried out, "It's a ghost!"
But Jesus spoke to them at once. "Don't be afraid," he said.
"Take courage. I am here!"
(MATTHEW 14:26–27)

Last time, we read that Jesus had a hard and crazy day. He stayed behind to
pray while the disciples sailed over the lake, and they found another storm
on the way. In the middle of that storm and the middle of the lake, Jesus
decided to catch up . . . on foot!

Naturally, the disciples were a tiny bit afraid. Oops, did I say a tiny bit?
Actually, I meant out-of-their-minds terrified. Can you blame them? I mean,
when was the last time you saw a person take a stroll across a lake while
the wind whistled and wailed, darkness blotted out the shore, and clouds
dumped buckets of water all around you? Yikes!

Jesus wanted them to have peace, so he called out to them not to be afraid.
I don't know about you, but normally when people say to me, "Don't be
afraid," it doesn't help very much. But Jesus didn't lecture them. He told them
why they didn't need to be afraid.

Did you notice what he said? "Take courage. I am here." That seems like
a fairly obvious statement, but that little phrase "I am here" would have
reminded the disciples of two important verses from the Old Testament.

They would have known Job 9:8, which says, "He alone has spread out
the heavens and marches on the waves of the sea." Here was Jesus, walking
on the waves of the sea, something only God can do. Jesus was showing the
disciples that he is God.

Second, Jesus said, "I am." That might not seem like a big deal, except for
a very important part of the Old Testament.

One day, God talked to a man named Moses from a burning bush. Moses wanted to know whom he was talking to, so God told him his name: I AM. This is the same God who created the world and eventually helped rescue an entire nation of people from slavery. He's amazingly powerful.

Later, Jesus used this same phrase, and people tried to kill him because they knew he was basically saying, "I am God." When he was being arrested, he said, "I am he," to a group of soldiers, and it knocked them flat on their backs because of the power of the name!

Jesus's disciples could take courage and have peace because I AM—the powerful God—was with them. They were not alone.

And guess what? You can have peace too because I AM is with you. When you're worried that you don't fit in, struggling with your schoolwork, or something bad is happening at home, remember this: the same God who walked on water and comforted his disciples can bring you peace too.

DISCUSSION STARTER

- In both of these storm stories, Jesus makes the storm go away. Does he always make the hard things in our lives go away? Why or why not?
- Is there something in your life right now that feels like a storm? If so, what is it?

PRAYER

Thank you, Jesus, that you are peace. Help us to trust you more with each life storm we go through. Amen.

DAY 35

COURAGEOUS PEACE

Then Peter called to him, "Lord, if it's really you,
tell me to come to you, walking on the water."
"Yes, come," Jesus said.
So Peter went over the side of the boat and walked on the
water toward Jesus. But when he saw the strong wind and the
waves, he was terrified and began to sink.
"Save me, Lord!" he shouted.
Jesus immediately reached out and grabbed him.
(MATTHEW 14:28–31)

Some things just go together, like peanut butter and jelly, salt and pepper, campfires and s'mores. You know what else goes together? Peace and courage.

We've been learning how Jesus can bring peace even when things are super scary, like when you're in the middle of a storm on a huge lake in a rickety boat. Having peace in your heart is lovely, but Jesus doesn't just want us to sit around being happy and peaceful. He gives us peace for a purpose: so we can have courage.

Courage is the strength to act even when you're scared. It's something God gives you. Imagine you are scared of going into a dark basement. Eek! I'm even scared of that sometimes, and I'm an adult! When you pray, God can give you peace, which is the feeling that no matter what you do or where you go, he is with you. That feeling is like a bubble of peace surrounding you. Now that you've got peace, you can walk down to the basement. That's courage.

This is what happened with Peter. Jesus had this bubble of amazing peace around him. Peter could walk on water because he knew God had given him the power to do it. Peter hopped over the side of the boat and had a peace bubble just like Jesus—until he looked at the waves around him and his bubble POPPED.

Maybe you're afraid of sleeping away from your parents. Maybe you're afraid to do something kind for a kid you don't get along with. Or maybe you're scared to tell someone when you're hurting inside. When you look at what's happening around you, it can easily pop your peace bubble.

When Peter took his eyes off Jesus, he noticed the storm around him. The wind and waves had been there the whole time, but because he suddenly focused on them instead of on Jesus, Peter lost his peace and sank. When we only look at the bad things in our lives, we become anxious and afraid. But when we look at Jesus and all the amazing works he's done for us, that peace comes back. And just like campfires naturally lead to s'mores, peace naturally leads to courage: courage to sleep away from home, courage to be kind, courage to talk to the people who love you.

DISCUSSION STARTER

- What is something courageous you have done? Were you peaceful or afraid while you did it?
- What amazing things has Jesus done for you?

PRAYER

Please show us how to receive your peace, Jesus, so we can have courage every day. Amen.

DAY 36

GRATEFUL PEACE

"I am leaving you with a gift—peace of mind and heart. And the peace I give is a gift the world cannot give. So don't be troubled or afraid."

(JOHN 14:27)

If you've ever set up a toy train track, you've probably set it up in a circle or oval. Then you push the toy train around the circle again, and again, and again. No matter what, the train can't get off that looping track.

Having a lot of worries can feel just like riding a toy train around a track. You keep thinking the same thoughts over and over again, and it can feel impossible to get off the worry track. Maybe you have so many worries and fears about school that you're super stressed out, or you're so worried about the monster under the bed that you can't go to sleep. Or maybe you keep thinking about a friend who doesn't seem to like you anymore. There are lots of things that can make our minds drive around in circles.

Now imagine that someone comes along and replaces one of your track pieces with a switching track. Instead of going around and around, now you have the choice to get off the circle and drive somewhere else. That's what peace is like.

You might be wondering how to actually get off that circular track when you're anxious and afraid. The Bible tells us just what to do: "Don't worry about anything; instead, pray about everything. Tell God what you need, and thank him for all he has done" (Philippians 4:6).

You talk to God about it, tell him what you need, and (here's the secret) thank him. Did you know that when you are grateful, you have a harder time being anxious?

Saying thanks to Jesus is like choosing the switching track that he's laid down for you. The more you thank Jesus for what he has done, the more he can fill your mind with peace, and "his peace will guard your hearts and minds as you live in Christ Jesus" (Philippians 4:7).

Jesus told us not to be troubled or afraid, and he gave us someone to help because he knew most of us have a hard time switching mind tracks by ourselves.

To help, he gives us the Holy Spirit. Jesus said, "But when the Father sends the Advocate as my representative—that is, the Holy Spirit—he will teach you everything and will remind you of everything I have told you" (John 14:26).

The Holy Spirit's job is to remind us that true peace comes only from God, and that the best way to feel it is to start giving thanks for what he's given us.

DISCUSSION STARTER

- What makes you anxious and afraid?
- Let's make a list of ten things we can thank God for.

PRAYER

God, we are worried about many things. Thank you for the gift of peace. Help us to open the gift through gratitude. Amen.

DAY 37

BACKSTAGE PEACE

"The time is coming—indeed it's here now—when you will be
scattered, each one going his own way, leaving me alone. Yet I
am not alone because the Father is with me. I have told you all
this so that you may have peace in me. Here on earth you will
have many trials and sorrows. But take heart, because I have
overcome the world."

(JOHN 16:32–33)

Have you ever watched a "behind the scenes" feature after a movie? They
normally include interviews with the actors, information on how special
effects are done, and sneak peeks of future movies. It's neat to see all the different parts of creating a movie and how they're put together.

In this conversation between Jesus and his disciples, he let them peek
behind the scenes, just for a bit. He gave them a sneak peek of what was going
to happen, and it wasn't going to be good. He said they would abandon him
and run away from each other.

I wonder if any of his disciples shook their heads in confusion, after Jesus
spoke these words to them. It seems like Jesus said, "You're going to run
away from me. Life is going to stink. So have a nice life!" It seems a little
smart-alecky, doesn't it?

But actually, this sneak peek would bring them peace. See, Jesus wanted
them to know that *he* already knew they would screw up. He wouldn't be
surprised when they all ran away from him at his arrest. Later, his disciples
would remember this "sneak peek" and know that he still loved them.

Does it bring you some peace to know that you can't surprise Jesus either?
No matter how badly you mess up, Jesus isn't surprised. He isn't shocked at
our mistakes and bad decisions.

Imagine that you lied to your teacher or parents and got in huge trouble because of the lie. God didn't throw up his hands and say, "Oh man! What a crummy kid! I give up on that one." No way. God has promised to always be with you, no matter how many mistakes you make. When God looks at you, he sees his precious child, not a crummy kid. He wants to take all your mess-ups and help you learn from them so you can become more like his Son, Jesus.

The next time you make a mistake, remember that God won't ever abandon you. He knew it was going to happen, and he's working behind the scenes to help you learn and grow.

DISCUSSION STARTER

- If you could get a sneak peek of the future, what would you want to see?
- How does the promise of "trials and sorrows" bring peace?

PRAYER

God, there are a lot of trials and sorrows in our world right now and even in our family. I praise you because you are bigger and stronger than the trouble. Help us to find peace in you! Amen.

DAY 38

TRUSTWORTHY PEACE

"Don't let your hearts be troubled. Trust in God, and
trust also in me."
(JOHN 14:1)

Has anyone in your family ever left you for a long trip? Maybe your mom
went to a conference, or your dad had to go away for work, or your grand-
parents went on a super long vacation. It doesn't feel great to be left behind,
does it?

The disciples were feeling the same way during the last supper they ate
with Jesus. He said, "I will be with you only a little longer. . . . You will search
for me, but you can't come where I am going" (John 13:33). It kind of sounds
like he was going to play an epic game of hide-and-seek, and he had found
the best hiding spot ever!

His disciples didn't want Jesus to leave them behind. Just like you might
want to keep your eyes partially open when your friends are hiding around
the room, Simon Peter sneakily asked, "Lord, where are you going?" (John
13:36). Peter wanted to know where Jesus's epic hiding spot was going to be
so he could find him.

Jesus didn't tell him. Instead, he just said, "You can't go with me now, but
you will follow me later" (John 13:36).

Peter was super whiny about it. "'But why can't I come now, Lord?' he
asked" (John 13:37). Thankfully, Jesus decided to reassure Peter rather than
roll his eyes at him. He said, "Don't let your hearts be troubled. Trust in God,
and trust also in me" (John 14:1). He wanted his disciples to have peace in
their hearts, to trust that Jesus knew exactly what he was doing. He even gave
them a clue about where he would be going. He said he was going to prepare
a place for them in his Father's house, but then he'd be back to get them.

They didn't really understand at first, but Jesus had just told them that he was making a way for them to be together with him in heaven forever. Jesus's friends would look back on this conversation after his death and resurrection and realize what Jesus was talking about. Knowing that Jesus had a plan and that they'd be with him forever would bring them great peace for the rest of their lives.

These words can bring us peace too. We know that Jesus has a plan, and that we'll be with him forever. That means we don't need to be afraid of the future because Jesus is trustworthy.

DISCUSSION STARTER

- What is something about the future that makes you worried?
- Let's tell those worries to Jesus right now.

PRAYER

Jesus, thank you for being trustworthy. We know you have a plan for our lives, both on earth and in heaven. Please help us to be at peace, knowing that you've got everything under control. Amen.

DAY 39

PEACEFUL POSITION

The high priest stood up before the others and asked Jesus,
"Well, aren't you going to answer these charges? What do you
have to say for yourself?" But Jesus was silent and made no reply.
(MARK 14:60–61)

Have you ever heard the phrase "kangaroo court"? A kangaroo is an
Australian animal that makes huge jumps, so a kangaroo court is a trial that
jumps. The trial might jump out of nowhere by suddenly arresting someone
without proof, or it might jump over evidence that would help the accused
person. A kangaroo court is always completely unfair to the person on trial.

When the religious leaders arrested Jesus, he was definitely in a kangaroo
court. Trials were supposed to happen in the daytime, in a public place, but
they arrested him at night and brought him to the chief priest's home for
trial. As well, the leaders jumped from witness to witness, actively looking
for fake evidence they could bring against Jesus. They weren't trying to find
out the truth. They were trying to find an excuse to get rid of Jesus.

Through all of this, Jesus was silent. He didn't defend himself, even
though a lot of what they said wasn't true. How would you react if someone
was accusing you of something untrue? I would definitely argue back! Why
didn't Jesus argue with them or blast them with some holy fire or something
else that showed who he really was?

Jesus knew the plan—he would die, and God would use his death to save
the world. Because his death would mean we could be his family, Jesus didn't
feel the need to yell and argue and defend himself. He might still have been
scared, but he was at peace, because he knew this was part of God's plan.

But there was also another reason he didn't fight against this kangaroo
court.

When the high priest asked Jesus if he was the promised one God sent to save his people, Jesus said, "I am." And then he said, "You will see the Son of Man seated in the place of power at God's right hand and coming on the clouds of heaven" (Mark 14:62). Wow, did that take guts. Back then, claiming to be God was a death sentence.

Jesus was also at peace with who he was; he didn't need to convince others that he was the Son of God, because he absolutely knew, without a shadow of doubt, that he was God's Son.

It's a lot easier for us to live in peace when we know who we are. Do you know who you are? You're a child of God! You're not likely to be dragged into court at midnight, but when the bully, bad test score, disease, or bad attitude comes along, remember that you are a child of God, and nothing can take that away from you.

DISCUSSION STARTER

- Has anyone ever accused you of doing something you didn't do? How did you react?
- Who are you? Think of some ways to describe who you are in Christ.

PRAYER

Thank you, Jesus, for showing us that when we know exactly who we are in you, we don't have to overreact to people who try to hurt us. Please help us be so strong in our identity that we have peace in our hearts. Amen.

DAY 40

TRUSTING PEACE

The two from Emmaus told their story of how Jesus had
appeared to them as they were walking along the road, and how
they had recognized him as he was breaking the bread. And just
as they were telling about it, Jesus himself was suddenly
standing there among them. "Peace be with you," he said.
(LUKE 24:35–36)

Have you ever heard someone wonder if Jesus *really* rose from the dead?
Maybe you had a family dinner at Easter and someone said it wasn't possible
for Jesus to come back to life, or a friend asked if the resurrection was true.
Questions like that can make you anxious sometimes.

The apostle Paul wrote, "If Christ has not been raised, then all our preaching is useless, and your faith is useless" (1 Corinthians 15:14). Yikes! We don't
want a useless faith.

Here's some ways we can know that Jesus really did come back to life.

1. *Jesus really did die.* Obviously this is what the Bible says, but other
   authors from Jesus's time tell us that everyone believed Jesus had
   really, truly died and was buried. That means he didn't just get better
   and stagger out of the tomb.
2. *Jesus's disciples believed he came back to life and that they saw him.* Over
   five hundred people saw him at different times. They touched him
   and ate with him. Jesus's followers believed he was truly alive and
   not a ghost or a hallucination. Otherwise, they wouldn't have told
   everyone they knew about his resurrection and even died for the
   gospel. If they were pretending to have seen Jesus, they wouldn't
   have been willing to die for the lie.
3. *Jesus's empty tomb was first seen by women.* This doesn't seem like such

a strange thing, except that people in this ancient culture didn't believe women were trustworthy. If Jesus's disciples were making up a story about Jesus's resurrection, they would definitely have said that men were the first to see Jesus's empty tomb, not women.

4. *Paul and James were suddenly changed.* Paul killed Christians because he thought they were horrible people, until he met Jesus for real and he became a powerful missionary. Jesus's brother James also didn't believe that his brother was God's Son until he met the resurrected Jesus. After that, he followed Jesus and became the leader of the Christians in Jerusalem.

What does all this mean for you and me? Well, it means that Jesus really is alive! You can believe the Bible and feel at peace about God's plan even when Uncle Frank or your friends ask tough questions. You could even share some of these proofs with them. Who knows? Maybe it will help them accept the peace that Jesus brings too!

DISCUSSION STARTER

- Which of the evidences for the resurrection helps you understand it the best?

PRAYER

Jesus, thank you for being alive! Please take the truths about peace that we have learned and plant them deep in our hearts so they grow the fruit of peace in our lives. Amen.

PATIENCE

HANDS-ON GROWTH ACTIVITIES

Use these activities as a hands-on supplement to the daily devotions. You can add in one per day, flip to this page for an idea only on days when you have a few extra minutes, or use a few of the activities each Sunday.

Memorize it: Memorize Ephesians 4:2 together over the next two weeks.

Write it: Write Ephesians 4:2 in big block letters. Hang it on your wall.

Draw it: Divide your paper in half. On one side, draw a picture of something that makes you impatient. On the other side, draw a picture of a way you make others impatient. Thank God for being so patient with you!

Pray it: Pray a breath prayer: As you breathe in, say, "Jesus Christ, Son of God . . ." and as you breathe out, say, "give me patience."

Research it: How many times can you find in the Old Testament where God had patience with the people of Israel?

Imagine it: Close your eyes and imagine that someone is driving you up-the-wall crazy. Now imagine that Jesus is beside you. What does he do that helps you have patience?

Play it: Using family members or stuffed animals, act out one of the Bible passages from the Patience section of this book.

Sing it: Make up a song about God's patience, using the memory verse.

Ask it: What would be different if our God wasn't a patient God?

Speak it: Practice saying Ephesians 4:2 while everyone else in your family jumps and yells around you.

For Bible verse printables and other activities,
please visit fruitofthespiritbook.com.

DAY 41

REMOTE PATIENCE

As soon as Jesus heard the news, he left in a boat to a remote
area to be alone. But the crowds heard where he was headed and
followed on foot from many towns. Jesus saw the huge crowd as
he stepped from the boat, and he had compassion on them and
healed their sick.
(MATTHEW 14:13–14)

Jesus was in a remote place, which means he was far away from any town. Do
you know why he was there?

Jesus had just been told that his cousin John the Baptist had been beheaded
by King Herod. That's pretty awful.

Have you ever lost someone you loved? It makes you feel like someone has
punched a hole in your insides, making you tired and sad and grumpy and
even worried.

The Bible doesn't say that Jesus was sad, but it does say that as soon as
Jesus heard the news, he left in a boat to a remote place to be alone. Jesus was
probably feeling all those feelings I mentioned. He wanted to be alone, but
the crowds figured out where he was going, and they chased the boat.

Have you ever just wanted to be alone for a while? Maybe you were sad,
or frustrated, or disappointed, and you went into your room to be alone, but
someone followed you. It's hard to be patient with people when we're in a
mood like that, isn't it?

I bet you've seen the word *remote* before, but it meant something else. Have
you ever used a remote for a TV? A remote can be used to change the volume
from far away. When I'm upset, I'd often like to use a remote on the people
in my life and turn down the volume of their voices. Unfortunately, remotes
don't work like that!

In this story, Jesus could have pretended he had a remote: he could have hopped back in the boat and stayed in the middle of the lake. It would have been like turning off the TV and walking away. That's probably what I would have done! Instead, he got out of the boat and started serving them, even though he was terribly sad.

Jesus's reaction shows us that even when you have a crummy day and you just want to hide in your room, but your little sister wants to play, it is possible to be patient with her. Or when you just had a fight with a friend, and then you have to answer a math question, it is possible to be patient. When the Holy Spirit works in us, he helps us become more like Jesus, and that includes being patient even when we're feeling awful.

Would you like to grow in patience?

DISCUSSION STARTER

- Can you think of a time when you just wanted to be alone, but someone interrupted you? What did you do?
- Is there someone who always seems to want something from you?
- How can you show patience with that person this week? (Remember, "Ask God for help" is a great answer!)

PRAYER

Jesus, thank you for being patient even when you were sad. Please help us to become more like you and grow in patience no matter how we feel. Amen.

DAY 42

UNHURRIED LIFE

That evening the disciples came to him and said, "This is a
remote place, and it's already getting late. Send the crowds away
so they can go to the villages and buy food for themselves."
But Jesus said, "That isn't necessary—you feed them."
"But we have only five loaves of bread and two fish!"
they answered. "Bring them here," he said.
(MATTHEW 14:15–18)

There seem to be two kinds of people in the world: those who are always in
a hurry, and those who are never in a hurry. The hurried person is already
buckled into the car while their unhurried family member wanders around
dreamily, forgetting that they were supposed to find their shoes. What kind
of person are you?

In today's Bible passage, Jesus didn't seem to be in any hurry to go any-
where. He was in another remote place with his disciples and thousands of
followers. But it was getting late, and his disciples' stomachs were probably
grumbling. They were the kind of people with important schedules and no
time for lunch. If they'd had watches, they would have been tapping them,
saying, "Um, Jesus, it's getting late! Send these people home!" But instead of
snapping at the disciples or telling them to relax, Jesus gave them an impossible job. I imagine them giving each other The Look and whispering, "Did he
just say what I think he said?" and "But that was supposed to be our supper!"

The disciples weren't wrong. It really was late, and the logical thing to do
was to shoo the crowds away, but Jesus patiently chose to serve and show his
power.

The disciples weren't patient. But Jesus is always patient. He waited while
the disciples gathered the tiny lunch that could get the party started, then
took the time to pray and pass out food to over five thousand people. I'm so

glad Jesus was patient with his disciples, because otherwise we might never have had this amazing miracle.

Looking at Jesus always shows us something true about God. He is patient with us, even when we don't deserve it. So when you keep making the same mistake over and over, God is patient with you. When you can't seem to stop pestering your sister or telling lies or having grumpy days, God is patient with you. He isn't in a hurry. God knows that as you keep listening to him, he can help you change and grow the fruit of patience.

And guess what? If God is patient with you, you can be patient with yourself too. Keep getting to know God and he will patiently help you stop making that same mistake.

DISCUSSION STARTER
- When do you get impatient with yourself?
- What do you think God might say to people who are always impatient?

PRAYER
Jesus, thank you for your incredible patience with us. Please help us show patience to each other and to ourselves. Amen.

DAY 43

FRUSTRATING PATIENCE

Then the mother of James and John, the sons of Zebedee, came to
Jesus with her sons. She knelt respectfully to ask a favor. "What
is your request?" he asked. She replied, "In your Kingdom,
please let my two sons sit in places of honor next to you, one on
your right and the other on your left."
(MATTHEW 20:20–21)

Have you ever tried to explain something to someone and no matter how
much you tried, they still didn't understand? Maybe you were trying to
explain a scene in a video game to your mom, and no matter what you said,
she stayed confused. Or you tried to help your friend solve a math problem,
and he still couldn't figure it out. It's frustrating, right? When someone just
doesn't get what we're trying to say, it can make us want to pull our hair out.
(Or their hair out. Yikes!)

Jesus experienced that a lot, and for a good reason. Jesus was and is God,
one of the Trinity, the mysterious three-in-one. He had God's wisdom and
plan and understanding in his brain, but unfortunately, no one else did.
People around him were always scratching their heads and arguing with
him and misunderstanding. Even his closest friends didn't get it!

In Matthew 20, James and John got their mom to ask Jesus a very important
(and totally rude) question. These guys were two of Jesus's closest friends.
Jesus's disciples were the ones who really seemed to get it. Except this time
. . . and many other times.

James and John's mom asked Jesus if he would let them sit on either side of
him when he became king. How do you think the other disciples reacted to
this question? They lost their tempers. I imagine their faces getting red under
their beards and Peter growling at James and John. *How dare they ask for such
a special privilege?* The other disciples were totally disgusted. They wanted
places of honor too!

Jesus looked right at James and John and said, "You don't know what you are asking!" (Matthew 20:22). Then he patiently explained a little bit about God's plan. He basically said, "There isn't going to be a fairy-tale coronation complete with balloons and golden-sprinkle cupcakes. And besides, no one gets to pick where they sit."

Don't worry, James and John eventually figured out that Jesus didn't come to earth in order to host fancy parties. But in the meantime, Jesus had to have mountain-sized amounts of patience with his disciples.

When someone asks us a crazy question, you and I can be either like the disciples or like Jesus. We can react out of our own frustration and impatience. Or we can take three seconds and ask Jesus to give us his patience. He loves answering prayers like that. When we honestly ask him, he gives us his very own patience to use. And then we can answer people with kindness rather than anger or frustration.

DISCUSSION STARTER

- Who makes you really impatient?
- How could we remind each other to take a breath and ask for God's patience when we're frustrated?

PRAYER

Thank you, Jesus, for your incredible patience with us. Please help us to remember to ask for your help when we get frustrated. Amen.

DAY 44

TESTING MY PATIENCE

Then the Pharisees met together to plot how to trap Jesus into
saying something for which he could be arrested. . . . But Jesus
knew their evil motives. "You hypocrites!" he said. "Why are you
trying to trap me?"
(MATTHEW 22:15, 18)

Have you ever known a kid who tried to get you in trouble even when you
weren't doing anything wrong? Jesus had that problem too. A lot of guys who
called themselves Pharisees were out to get Jesus for sure.

Worse. The Pharisees were the religious leaders of Israel. They taught the
people the story of Israel and God's laws. Even though we tend to think of
Pharisees as bad people, a lot of them simply wanted to know God more.

Some of the Pharisees understood that Jesus had come from God and
chose to follow him. But many of them didn't like Jesus at all. Jesus did a lot
of things they thought were against God's laws. For example, they knew it
was against God's laws to work on the Sabbath, so when Jesus healed a man
on the Sabbath, they were confused. Was it work or was it not? Was God
pleased or was he angry?

The Pharisees saw their people following this confusing man all over the
countryside, and they became afraid. They didn't want to lose their power,
and they certainly didn't want to get in trouble with the Romans, who ruled
Israel.

So they started acting like that mean kid in school. They pretended to
ask honest questions when they actually wanted to trick Jesus. They wanted
to force him to say something that would make the people of Israel or the
Romans hate him.

What would you do if you knew someone was trying to trick you and get
you in trouble? You and I might get annoyed, but Jesus calmly and patiently

answered their questions in a way that didn't make anyone hate him. It was a good answer for the Israelites and it was a good answer for the Romans. The only people who didn't like his answer were the Pharisees, and they were just mad that he didn't get in trouble.

It can be really hard to have patience when someone is trying to get you into trouble. But as Romans 8:12 reminds us, "You have no obligation to do what your sinful nature urges you to do." This verse means that even though you might want to lash out in anger, you don't have to. The Holy Spirit lives in you and gives you the power to be patient. We just have to ask! Isn't that an incredible gift?

DISCUSSION STARTER

- Tell about a time someone tried to get you in trouble.
- Let's create a phrase to say when we need to remember that the Holy Spirit will help us be patient.

PRAYER

Thank you, Jesus, for having such incredible patience with those who were trying to get you into trouble! Please fill us with your patience so we react wisely when others try to get us in trouble. Amen.

DAY 45

FORGETFULNESS

"Don't you remember the 5,000 I fed with five loaves, and the
baskets of leftovers you picked up? Or the 4,000 I fed with seven
loaves, and the large baskets of leftovers you picked up?"
(Matthew 16:9–10)

Imagine being an Israelite slave in Egypt for your whole life. You make bricks every day. No playground, no sports, no music lessons. Just bricks, bricks, and more bricks. You fall asleep with mud in your hair, then wake up and do it over again. Then one day your whole family and everyone you know is freed. You quickly pack up your few belongings and dance away from Egypt. It's a miracle!

You can definitely trust God now, right? But soon you are trapped between a sea of water and a sea of Egyptian soldiers. Will God really take care of you, or has he forgotten you? Your leader prays, and God answers by rolling up a cloud between you and the enemy. While you're all ogling the cloud, God opens the sea so you can walk right through it on dry land. Once everyone is across, the sea crashes back in and destroys the Egyptian army. It's a miracle!

You can definitely trust God now, right? But soon you get hungry. Will God really take care of you, or should you just head back to Egypt and its delicious leeks? After a lot of whining and complaining, your leader announces that every day there will be manna from heaven. God is feeding you. It's a miracle!

You can definitely trust God now, right? Well, soon you get thirsty. You are in the desert, after all. Will God really take care of you, or has he brought you here to die? After more complaining, your leader hits a rock with his staff, and enough water pours out for everyone to drink. It's a miracle!

Are you shocked at how quickly people forget what God has done? The disciples were the same. They witnessed Jesus feeding over four thousand people with seven loaves of bread and a couple fish, and a short time later they bickered over who forgot to bring bread.

Before you laugh at these silly people, remember that we often forget what God has done for us. We are just like the Israelites and the disciples. Sure, we don't often see such huge miracles, but God helps us be kind to an enemy, bite back mean words, or finish our math questions in time. Yet the next time we get into the same situation, we forget that God helped us.

It can be frustrating to keep forgetting what God has done for you. You might think you're a bad Christian because you don't always remember God. But God is just as patient with you as he was with the ancient Israelites and the disciples, and he can even help you be patient with yourself and your family as you all grow into stronger, more fruitful Christians.

DISCUSSION STARTER

- What is one cool thing God has done for you?
- What is one cool thing God has done for our family?

PRAYER

Thank you, Jesus, for being so patient with us, even when we forget you or forget what you've done. Please teach us to extend that kind of patience to others! Amen.

DAY 46

PATIENT QUESTIONING

"Don't you understand yet?" Jesus asked.
(MATTHEW 15:16)

Do you know someone who asks a lot of questions?

Jesus knew a little something about questions. Between his disciples, the people around him, and the religious leaders, he was asked 183 questions (that we know of). You might think he was great at giving answers, but guess how many of those 183 questions Jesus directly answered?

Three. Yup. Just three!

And in return, Jesus asked 307 questions of others. Turns out, Jesus gave a lot more questions than answers. He definitely knew the answers to the questions people asked, and he knew the answers to the questions he asked, but he used questions to help his followers learn.

Has anyone ever made you think that it was dangerous to ask God questions? If so, I'm sorry they made you feel that way, because that's not what Jesus shows us in the Bible. Jesus shows us that God welcomes our questions, and he might ask a few right back.

Asking God questions helps us think about our faith in new ways. For example, you might ask, "How can Jesus be the Son of God and God all at the same time?" That's a good question! Or you might ask, "If God really loves us, why do so many bad things happen?" That's a good question too.

Sometimes, Jesus's disciples totally didn't understand what he was trying to say to them. They missed the point and got confused and said weird, awkward stuff.

For example, Peter, James, and John got to see the most incredible thing happen to Jesus. They hiked up a mountain with him, and at the top, Jesus started blasting beams of light like the sun on a hot summer day. To top it off, they saw Moses and Elijah (who had been dead for a looooooong time) chatting with him. When they could finally see Jesus again, Peter babbled, "Lord, it's wonderful for us to be here! If you want, I'll make three shelters as memorials—one for you, one for Moses, and one for Elijah" (Matthew 17:4). Peter had totally missed the point. Jesus didn't bring them up there to stay or just to make fun memories. He brought them up there so they could understand that he truly is God's Son.

But guess what? Jesus isn't scared of what we might say or ask. He's incredibly patient with our wonderings and questions and wacky thoughts. He treats us just like he treated his disciples: with patience and love. He might shake his head and chuckle at our questions sometimes, but he's always gracious and understanding. Maybe someday one of your friends will ask you some questions about God that are wacky, or maybe your uncle will say something about the Bible that makes you confused. In that moment, take a deep breath, and ask the Holy Spirit to help you be patient with them, just like Jesus is patient with you.

DISCUSSION STARTER

- What's something you'd like to ask God, or something you wonder about God? Let's ask him our questions right now!

PRAYER

Thank you, Jesus, that you are so patient with our questions, and that you're not afraid of the weird things we say and think. Please help us to trust you with all our thoughts and questions. Amen.

DAY 47

PATIENT TIMING

The Lord isn't really being slow about his promise, as some
people think. No, he is being patient for your sake. He does not
want anyone to be destroyed, but wants everyone to repent.
(2 PETER 3:9)

What's the most agonizing wait you've ever had in your whole life? Maybe
you had to wait for your birthday because you knew you were going to get the
best present ever. Or maybe you were waiting for a vacation to Disneyland.
Or maybe the worst wait you ever had was when you were waiting in line
at an ice-cream party, and the kids in front of you were all using teeny, tiny
spoons to pile on the toppings. Phew! That all sounds super frustrating.
Sometimes we just have to wait for the right timing. We wait for our birthday,
or the right day to start the vacation, or the right moment when we can dig
into the ice-cream toppings.

Jesus had to wait for the right timing too.

Mark 1:34 says, "Jesus healed many people who were sick with various
diseases, and he cast out many demons. But because the demons knew who
he was, he did not allow them to speak." Why not? It wasn't the right timing. Jesus was kind of like a superhero with a secret identity. He didn't want
demons blabbing his true identity to the world because it might cause problems. It wasn't the right time to reveal his secret identity as the Son of God
and his secret mission to save the world.

After Jesus healed a deaf man, he told the whole crowd not to say anything. Why? This whole crowd now had a clue about his secret identity, but
they couldn't completely understand his identity or his mission. Jesus didn't
want them spreading rumors and getting him arrested before it was the right
time.

Finally, "Jesus knew that his hour had come to leave this world and return to his Father" (John 13:1). After three years of preaching and healing, Jesus was ready for the last part of his secret mission: to be arrested, killed, buried, and resurrected.

Often, it seems like God's timing makes no sense. If you've ever asked for something through prayer and not received the answer right away, you know what I mean. Sometimes God seems to wait a very long time to answer our prayers.

When Jesus died, the disciples probably thought God's timing was terrible. He didn't come back to life for three days! He knew his friends would be sad and confused, but he stayed dead until the right time.

Sometimes God's timing is confusing. But a huge part of growing in patience is learning to trust that God has a plan, even if we don't understand it. God's plan is good, and we can trust him.

DISCUSSION STARTER

- What makes you feel impatient today?
- What prayer have you prayed that seems unanswered?

PRAYER

Jesus, thank you for showing us what it looks like to wait for God's timing. Please help us trust that you have a plan, even if we don't understand it. Amen.

DAY 48

PATIENCE IN CONFUSION

That same day two of Jesus' followers were walking to the
village of Emmaus, seven miles from Jerusalem. As they walked
along they were talking about everything that had happened.
As they talked and discussed these things, Jesus himself
suddenly came and began walking with them.
But God kept them from recognizing him.
(LUKE 24:13–16)

Has anyone ever thrown you a surprise birthday party? If not, here's how
it works. Everyone prepares the party without telling you anything. Your
family makes the cake, invites the guests, and plans silly party games, all
so they can show you how much you are loved! People don't throw surprise
parties to be mean. They throw surprise parties as a way to show you how
much you are loved.

In the verses we read today, two of Jesus's followers were going for a walk
on the day of Jesus's resurrection. Only, they didn't know it was a special day
yet. It was a surprise. Even when Jesus joined them, he didn't tell them who he
was. God specifically kept them from recognizing Jesus, kind of like if your
dad made you wear a blindfold in the car on the way to your surprise party.

Jesus pretended not to know anything about his own death, so his friends
told him all about it. This would be like if your dad pretended to be driving
you to the dentist because he forgot all about your birthday. Then, like your
dad starting a conversation about all your previous birthday parties, Jesus
reminded his friends about all the things written in the Old Testament. They
talked like this all the way to Emmaus, then sat down for dinner together.

"As they sat down to eat, he took the bread and blessed it. Then he broke it
and gave it to them. Suddenly, their eyes were opened, and they recognized
him. And at that moment he disappeared!" (Luke 24:30–31).

Those disciples sure got a surprise! Can you imagine if you got to your surprise birthday party and Jesus was standing there with a slice of cake? Wow! I don't think you could possibly be more surprised than these two friends were right then. They had thought Jesus was dead, but he had actually been walking with them, explaining Scripture to them.

Sometimes you might get confused about Jesus too. When bad things happen to you, like a friend moves away, someone special dies, or you feel like you just don't understand math, it's normal to start wondering if God is really with you and if he really does care about you. You might find yourself wondering if anyone really cares about you at all, like when everyone is being secretive and won't talk to you before your big surprise party.

You can trust that Jesus comes alongside you, patiently teaching you to trust him even when life is hard or confusing. Keep your eyes open, and patiently wait for what he might do in your life. He might teach you that he is your best friend, or he might comfort you in sadness, or he might help you understand math. No matter what, God has wonderful surprises in store for your life. You just need to keep your eyes open for them!

DISCUSSION STARTER

- Have you ever wondered if God really is with you? If so, when?

PRAYER

Thank you, Jesus, for your gentle patience when we are confused about you. You are so gentle and patient with us. Please help us be patient with you as you help us grow and become more like you. Amen.

DAY 49

PATIENCE WITH UNBELIEF

One of the twelve disciples, Thomas (nicknamed the Twin), was
not with the others when Jesus came. They told him, "We have
seen the Lord!" But he replied, "I won't believe it unless I see the
nail wounds in his hands, put my fingers into them, and place
my hand into the wound in his side."
(JOHN 20:24–25)

There are many things we believe in even though we can't see them with the
naked eye. We believe in germs and black holes, that the earth is round, and
that dinosaurs used to roam the earth.

With a good microscope, you can see germs, and we all know what germs
do to our bodies. We know the earth is round because astronauts have gone
into space and taken pictures of it. We know that dinosaurs lived because
paleontologists have discovered bones, footprints, and even fossilized poo.
Astronomers can't actually see black holes with their telescopes, but we
believe they exist because mathematicians and other scientists have calculated
that black holes are the reason for many strange events that occur in space.

Science tells us a lot about our world, but there are some things science
can't explain. For example, science can't explain how a man who was completely and utterly dead could come back to life.

In today's verses, we met a man often nicknamed "Doubting Thomas." He
wasn't around when the disciples first saw the risen Jesus, so he just couldn't
believe it. There was no proof. No one had ever come back to life on their own
before. He doubted they were telling the truth.

When we talk about these verses, we usually assume Jesus was mad at
Thomas for doubting. But instead of getting angry, Jesus let Thomas put his
fingers into the nail marks. He was patient even with Thomas's doubts. He
knew that Thomas needed a bit of evidence in order to believe.

How about you? Do you ever have trouble believing in a God you can't see? Luckily, you're in good company. After encountering Jesus, Thomas became the very first person to call Jesus "God." Afterward, Thomas ended up being an incredible missionary, sharing the good news of Jesus all the way to India.

As you grow up, you will meet people who don't believe God exists or that the Bible is true. That can be really hard and sometimes scary. But guess what? God doesn't get all panicky about it. Your doubts don't scare him, and neither do anyone else's doubts. God is God whether people believe in him or not. If you meet someone who doesn't know Jesus yet, ask the Holy Spirit to help you be patient with them. You might be surprised at how the Holy Spirit can use your faith to help someone else believe in what they can't see.

DISCUSSION STARTER

- Have you ever doubted something about the Bible? (Parents, please share too! Then, invite members of your family to share any thoughts they have about each other's doubts. Make sure to be kind and patient with each other!)

PRAYER

Thank you, Jesus, for being patient with those who doubt. Teach us to trust you deeper as we learn to believe without seeing. Amen.

DAY 50

ROCK-SOLID PATIENCE

. After breakfast Jesus asked Simon Peter, "Simon son of John, do
you love me more than these?" "Yes, Lord," Peter replied,
"you know I love you."
(JOHN 21:15)

Have you ever messed up? Maybe you said something so mean that you
ruined a friendship, slammed your door so hard that your dad took it off its
hinges, or talked back so bad to your mom that you lost all your privileges
for two weeks.

We all mess up sometimes, including Jesus's disciples. Take Peter, for
example.

Peter was one of Jesus's three best friends. He was the only disciple to
walk on water and was one of the first people to call Jesus Messiah. Jesus
said to Peter, "Now I say to you that you are Peter (which means 'rock'), and
upon this rock I will build my church, and all the powers of hell will not con-
quer it" (Matthew 16:18). What an amazing promise! It must have made Peter
stand up a lot straighter and cast a few side glances at his friends. "See?" he
might have thought, "I rock."

Peter was so convinced he was Jesus's best follower that he said he'd never,
ever, ever leave Jesus. Even if everyone else abandoned Jesus, he never would.
Peter knew he was a rock-solid best friend.

Except, this rock-solid friend ended up melting like hot lava the minute
Jesus was arrested. When people asked if he knew Jesus, Peter angrily denied
their friendship! Some rock he turned out to be.

You know who wasn't surprised that Peter messed up? Jesus. He knew
this was going to happen and even predicted that Peter would deny him
three times before the rooster crowed. Of course, it turned out exactly as he
said. Peter faked not knowing Jesus three times, then the rooster crowed. As

soon as Peter heard the bird, he knew how bad he had messed up and cried big, fat tears of regret.

Days later, Peter was again with Jesus, this time with a lot less self-confidence. Thankfully, Jesus has rock-solid patience with sinners like Peter. He gave Peter three chances to say, "I love you," and reminded him that he still had a place in God's kingdom.

Looking at Jesus always shows us something true about God. Jesus was patient with Peter and forgave him for ditching Jesus when he most needed a friend, and he will also forgive you when you mess up. As you become more like Jesus, he will help you be patient with your friends and family when they hurt you. Maybe you were having a rough morning and your mom yelled at you instead of finding out what was wrong. Jesus can help you show patience with her. Maybe your friend forgot she was supposed to meet you after soccer and you stood there lonely. Jesus can help you show patience with her too. When you show patience to people who mess up, you are showing them what Jesus looks like, and that can change someone's life.

DISCUSSION STARTER

- Tell about a time you messed up. (Feel free to refresh each other's memories if necessary!)
- Tell about a time you forgave someone who hurt you.

PRAYER

Thank you for your rock-solid patience, Jesus! Please take the truths we have learned and plant them deep in our hearts so they grow the fruit of patience in our lives. Amen.

KINDNESS

HANDS-ON GROWTH ACTIVITIES

Use these activities as a hands-on supplement to the daily devotions. You can add in one per day, flip to this page for an idea only on days when you have a few extra minutes, or use a few of the activities each Sunday.

Memorize it: Memorize Ephesians 4:32 together over the next two weeks.

Write it: Write out Ephesians 4:32 in bubble letters and hang it on your wall.

Draw it: Draw a picture of someone showing kindness. It could be a Bible story, a scene from a book, or something that happened in your life.

Pray it: Pray a breath prayer. As you breathe in, say, "Your kindness, Lord . . ." and as you breathe out, say, "leads me to you."

Research it: Brainstorm ideas of true stories from the Bible where someone showed kindness, then look up at least one of them.

Imagine it: The devotions in this section talk about Jesus's gut-wrenching compassion. What do you think that feels like? Act out the way you might feel if you experienced this kind of intense compassion.

Play it: As a family, ask God whom he would like you to show extra kindness to this week. Come up with a plan to show as many random acts of kindness to that person as you possibly can.

Sing it: Find (or make up) a song about God's kindness.

Ask it: What would be different if our God wasn't a kind God?

Speak it: Say Ephesians 4:32 as if you were speaking to someone very small and weak.

For Bible verse printables and other activities, please visit fruitofthespiritbook.com.

DAY 51

GUT-WRENCHING COMPASSION

A funeral procession was coming out as he approached the village gate. The young man who had died was a widow's only son, and a large crowd from the village was with her. When the Lord saw her, his heart overflowed with compassion. "Don't cry!" he said.

(LUKE 7:12–13)

Imagine something really awful happening to your best friend. What is awful enough to make your friend cry all day? (Remember, it's not actually going to happen, we're just imagining.) Maybe their dog got run over, or their parents got divorced. You might be feeling really bad right now, because you don't want that awful thing to happen to them. In fact, you might even be feeling a bit sick. Ugh, what a miserable feeling! Do you know what that feeling is called? It's *compassion*. Having compassion for someone means that you feel really, really, really bad for someone. Sometimes we use the phrase "gut-wrenching" for this feeling because it makes you feel kind of sick to your stomach.

Now that you have an idea of what gut-wrenching compassion feels like, you know how Jesus felt when he met the funeral party. In the verses we just read, the phrase "overflowed with compassion" comes from the hard-to-pronounce Greek word *splanchnizomai* (splawnk-NITZ-oh-my). Try saying that three times, fast! This word is sometimes translated "compassion" or "had pity," but it all comes from the Greek word which means, "He felt it in his guts." Sounds gross, right?

When Jesus came upon that funeral party, he didn't say, "Oh, that's so sad." Instead, he felt that sick feeling in his stomach. He knew the woman had no hope for her future now that her husband and son were both dead. No one feels gut-wrenching compassion quite like Jesus.

That's what true kindness is all about. You might think kindness is just about "being nice," but that's not where it starts. True kindness is about letting yourself feel the same kind of painful sympathy that Jesus felt and then doing something about the problem. That's what Jesus did. He felt her pain, then fixed it by raising her son from the dead!

Of course, we can't raise someone from the dead, and it sometimes feels like you can't do anything about the things that are wrong in this world. The first thing to do is ask God to help you feel his compassion for the person.

When you feel true compassion, God will show you what to do next. He might ask you to hug a friend, or make some cookies for a neighbor . . . even just sit quietly with someone who's sad. Through Jesus, you have the power to bring life-changing kindness to your world.

DISCUSSION STARTER

- When you think about how God feels about you, what feelings do you normally think of?
- Is there someone you feel compassion for today? How could your feelings of compassion lead to an act of kindness?

PRAYER

Thank you, Jesus, for your gut-wrenching compassion for us. Please fill us with that same compassion for others and show us how to turn that compassion into kindness. Amen.

DAY 52

RUNNING COMPASSION

•

"He returned home to his father. And while he was still a long
way off, his father saw him coming. Filled with love and
compassion, he ran to his son, embraced him, and kissed him."
(LUKE 15:20)

Do you remember that funny Greek word we learned last time? *Splanchnizomai*
(splawnk-NITZ-oh-my) refers to the feeling Jesus had when he felt really bad
for someone, or when he "felt something in his guts." That doesn't mean he
ate a bad piece of meat but that he felt so badly for someone, it was like love
kicked him in the stomach or rolled his intestines into a ball. (Ouch!)

I wanted to remind you of this, because when you read the Bible verse
above, you might have thought, "Oh, that's nice, he felt love and compassion,"
like it was no big deal. Do you know where these verses come from? It's part
of one of the stories Jesus told to show us what God is like. In it, a rude son
demands a lot of money from his dad, then runs away and spends it on parties. Finally, there's nothing left to eat. He's living in rags and is so hungry
he wants to eat pig food. He decides to come home and beg for a place as a
servant in his father's house. He knows he doesn't deserve love anymore.
He's been absolutely horrible.

But when his father spies him out the window, he is filled with love and
compassion, and it is a really big deal. The father should never have let his
son back in the house after what he did. Instead, he felt his son's pain like a
punch to the gut, and his gut-wrenching compassion led him to welcome his
son back with open arms. Oh, and he also threw a party!

Jesus's stories always showed something true about God or God's kingdom, and this story shows how God treats us. God our Father runs toward us
like a father filled with gut-wrenching compassion, ready to show kindness.

Does it seem strange that God would have compassion for you? I bet it seemed strange to the son when his dad came running to hug him. He had basically said to his dad, "I wish you were dead!" That's not a great way to get people to feel compassion for you. But just like the father always loved his son, your heavenly Father always loves you and is just waiting to show kindness when you turn to him with your problems.

But Jesus doesn't show you kindness just for your sake. He doesn't want you to accept all his kindness, then turn around and be rude and unkind to others. The point of Jesus showing kindness to you is so you can then turn around and show unexpected kindness to someone else. Maybe you know a boy no one else likes because he's rude and obnoxious. Ask God to fill you with compassion for this kid. When you do that, you might remember that the boy's parents aren't very nice to him, or that he hasn't learned how to read yet, so he feels embarrassed in class. When you feel compassion for someone, it's a whole lot easier to pass on God's kindness, even to people who don't seem to deserve it.

DISCUSSION STARTER

- Tell about a time someone was kind to you when you didn't deserve it.
- Tell about a time you were kind to someone who didn't deserve it.

PRAYER

Thank you, God, for showing us how compassionate and kind you are. Thank you for showing compassion and kindness to us when we least deserve it. Amen.

DAY 53

FULL OF COMPASSION

Jesus called his disciples and told them, "I feel sorry for these people. They have been here with me for three days, and they have nothing left to eat. I don't want to send them away hungry, or they will faint along the way."
(MATTHEW 15:32)

Do you remember that long Greek word we've been learning? It's *splanchnizomai* (splawnk-NITZ-oh-my), or let's say *splank* for short. It's used in the Bible for times when Jesus experienced gut-wrenching compassion for someone.

In fact, it's used in today's verse. In this translation, Jesus says, "I feel sorry for these people," which doesn't quite get to the meaning of the original Greek word. Jesus experienced gut-wrenching compassion for the crowd because they had been with him for three days and didn't have anything to eat. He was worried they might collapse if he sent them away without food.

But Jesus didn't just feel *splank*, then shrug his shoulders and send them away. No way! Jesus saw something that was wrong, let himself be deeply moved by it, then chose to do something about it. In this case, he did an incredible miracle. Jesus took seven loaves of bread and a few small fish and multiplied them so they fed thousands of people. They even had seven basketfuls of leftovers!

Do you think we can experience *splank* too? It's a feeling that seems to belong only to Jesus. But we know that Jesus's Spirit lives inside us, helping us become more like him, so God can move us to gut-wrenching compassion too. God doesn't give us *splank* just to make us feel bad. The reason God sometimes gives us that feeling is so, just like Jesus, we can choose kindness. That feeling can remind us that something is wrong with the world, and God is calling us to do something about it.

For example, have you ever seen someone who needs food? Maybe you've seen homeless people on the street or a kid in your class who doesn't have lunch. Most people choose to turn away from hungry people because they don't know what to do about it. But if God gives you a feeling of compassion for a hungry person, he will also give you a way to help. Maybe you'll have a granola bar you can share with a kid at school. Or maybe you can ask your mom to buy a sandwich for a hungry person on the street. Both of those are ways to show God's kindness.

DISCUSSION STARTER

- Have you ever felt compassion for someone but weren't exactly sure how to help?
- What are some ways that we could move from just *feeling* compassion for the hungry to actually *showing* kindness?

PRAYER

Jesus, thanks for showing your incredible compassion and kindness to so many people. Give us hearts of compassion, and show us how we can show kindness. Amen.

DAY 54

EYES OF KINDNESS

When Jesus heard them, he stopped and called,
"What do you want me to do for you?"
"Lord," they said, "we want to see!"
Jesus felt sorry for them and touched their eyes.
Instantly they could see! Then they followed him.
(MATTHEW 20:32–34)

Did you know that the only part of you that's more complicated than your eye is your brain? Everything else in your body, including your heart, lungs, and tongue, is way less complicated than your eyes. There are more than two million working parts in an eye that help us adjust to light and dark, see over ten million different shades of color, and so much more. Now, that's impressive. But sometimes eyes don't work like they're supposed to.

In today's passage, two men couldn't use their eyes at all. Can you imagine? In today's world there are things to help people who are blind, like helper dogs, audiobooks, and Braille to read. In ancient times, though, there weren't those helpful things, so someone who was blind couldn't get a job or raise a family. There was no such thing as guide dogs, or laser eye surgery, or even glasses. Blind people ended up as beggars, with no hope for a better life. These men sat by the side of the road every day, hoping that a rich person would notice them and give them some money so they could get something to eat.

One day a rich person did notice them, but not the kind of rich person they expected. It was Jesus, the homeless preacher who wandered from town to town, teaching and healing. He wasn't rich in money but was rich in love.

When these two blind men heard Jesus coming, they started shouting, "Lord, Son of David, have mercy on us!" The people around them got annoyed and shushed them. I guess they wanted to hear Jesus without being interrupted by two yelling beggars. But the blind men didn't stop. In fact, they shouted louder!

Finally, Jesus heard them. Thankfully, he didn't want to shush them because Jesus never shushes those who come to him for help. Jesus is never too busy to be compassionate and kind. When Jesus asked them what they wanted, they could have asked for riches or a safe home. But they didn't. They wanted their powerful, complex eyes to work properly. Jesus was gut-wrenched with compassion for these poor blind men. And what did Jesus do when he felt compassion for someone? He was kind! In this case, he fixed their sight.

Sometimes we behave just like that crowd. When a friend is struggling with a math problem, we don't help because we want to finish our own work early. Or maybe a friend doesn't have a marker to draw, but we don't want to loan him our favorite because we're afraid it will get lost or ruined. Or maybe we don't want to hold the door open for the girl on crutches in case we're late. When it comes down to it, we don't have compassion on those who are hurting because we don't understand them, or we are afraid of them, or we are too busy to help. But Jesus is always available to help us overcome our misunderstanding, fear, and busyness so we can be as kind as he is.

DISCUSSION STARTER

- Tell about a time when you didn't show kindness to someone because you were too busy or afraid.
- If the exact same thing happened tomorrow, how could God help you react differently?

PRAYER

Jesus, thank you that you always have time for people who are hurting. Please help me to see people with disabilities like you do. Amen.

DAY 55

CONTAGIOUS KINDNESS

Suddenly, a man with leprosy approached him and knelt before
him. "Lord," the man said, "if you are willing, you can heal me
and make me clean."
(MATTHEW 8:2)

When flu season hits, we wash our hands more, squirt sanitizer everywhere,
and sometimes even wear masks. We do this to keep ourselves clean and
germ free so we stay healthy.

In the Old Testament there were lots of rules about being clean and washing up, but they weren't all about germs. The rules said you weren't allowed
in the temple or even around the religious leaders unless you followed the
rules about washing up. It was important to follow all the washing-up rules
properly. It also helped if you could stay away from people and animals that
would make you "unclean" in the first place. There were a lot of things that
could make you unclean: touching a dead body or eating certain meats, like
geckos or pigs. And get this—if you touched someone who was unclean, you
also became unclean! Jewish people had to wash up in the exact right way
and with special water before they were allowed to go to the temple or offer
a sacrifice to God.

You know what else was considered unclean? A deadly disease called
leprosy. If you touched a person with leprosy, not only would you get their
germs, but it also meant you couldn't go to the temple and worship God.

In today's passage, a man with leprosy came close to Jesus and knelt before
him. The man knew Jesus could make him clean both ways: Jesus could heal
the leprosy and take away his uncleanness so he could worship God again.

Jesus reached out and touched him. That doesn't seem so earth-shattering,
does it? We reach out and touch people all the time. Except, do you think
Jesus *needed* to touch the man in order to heal him? We know he could heal

from a distance. Didn't he know that touching the leper would give him germs *and* make it so he wasn't allowed in the temple?

Of course he knew. But he didn't care. When Jesus reached out to touch that leper, he showed incredible kindness. In God's kingdom, it's more important to be compassionate and kind than to worry about staying clean.

Leprosy isn't a big deal in most parts of the world anymore, and Christians don't have any special rules about whom you can touch and whom you can't. But there are still people we don't like very much.

Imagine you're riding bikes with some neighborhood kids, and the girl who always has dirty clothes and a snotty nose keeps picking on you and calling you names. Ugh. But then she falls off her bike. You might get dirty or get some of her germs if you help her. But through God's power, he can help you feel compassion for her. And then, just like Jesus, you might go find her a bandage.

DISCUSSION STARTER

- Tell about a time someone was unkind to you.
- Tell about a time you were unkind to someone else. Let's brainstorm ways we can choose kindness in situations like that. (Remember to invite God into your brainstorm so he can guide you!)

PRAYER

Thank you, Jesus, for showing kindness to everyone, even people who are unkind. Please fill us with your compassion and kindness so we can love others like you do. Amen.

DAY 56

THE KINDEST ANGER

When Jesus saw her, he called her over and said, "Dear woman,
you are healed of your sickness!"
(LUKE 13:12)

Hunch your shoulders and look down at your belly button. Not a very inter-
esting view, is it. But there's a woman in the Bible whose body was stuck like
that for eighteen years. How long will it be before you are eighteen years old?
Can you imagine being bent double for your whole life, plus that many more
years? Living like that would be horrifying, but there was nothing anyone
could do for that poor woman.

One day, Jesus was teaching in a synagogue, which was like a church for
Jewish people. Suddenly, Jesus spotted this woman through the crowd.

I can imagine his heart breaking for her. This wasn't the way humans were
supposed to live. God created us to be whole and free and to dance and run
and laugh, but because of sin, our bodies hurt and break and get hunched
over. Jesus called her over and touched her. Instantly her backbone straight-
ened. For the first time in eighteen years, she could look someone in the eye.
I think she was probably crying her eyes out because she was so amazed and
grateful, and there were probably lots of other people crying too, because
Jesus's kindness and power were so incredible.

But there was one person who wasn't happy. The synagogue leader was
angry because it was the Sabbath day, and God's law said, "No working on
the Sabbath." To him, healing someone was work, so it was obviously against
the law. He gave the people a lecture, telling them to show up for healing the
rest of the week instead of the Sabbath.

Even though Jesus was always kind, he definitely got angry sometimes,
especially when someone tried to use God's laws to hurt others. He told the
synagogue leader that he was wrong. It is always right to free someone from

pain. Often when you and I get angry, it's a sinful, selfish anger. But Jesus's anger was part of his kindness. His heart was broken for this poor woman, and he knew that many of the religious leaders were heartless.

There's a lot of evil in our world, and with God's compassion inside us, we *should* get angry at the horrible ways that humans treat each other. Maybe you know that one of your friends is being hurt by an adult, or there's a bully on the playground. It's okay to be angry then. Jesus is angry too. You might think, "I'm just a kid. I can't do anything." But if you talk to God about it, he will help you know the best way to show kindness.

DISCUSSION STARTER

- What is something wrong in our world that makes you angry? Ask God if he wants you to do something about it.

PRAYER

Thank you, Jesus, for helping others even when you got in trouble. Please give us deep compassion for others and the right kind of anger against injustice, and show us how to help. Amen.

DAY 57

BEHIND ENEMY LINES

"Love your enemies! Do good to them. Lend to them without
expecting to be repaid. Then your reward from heaven will be
very great, and you will truly be acting as children of the Most
High, for he is kind to those who are unthankful and wicked."
(LUKE 6:35)

Have you ever had an enemy? Maybe it was someone who was mean to you,
or a buddy who stopped being your friend. It's impossible to be kind to an
enemy because, well, they're your enemy. Right? Well, let's see what Jesus
does.

Jesus's friends and family had a big, powerful enemy. Their enemy was
called Rome. The Romans lived far away but decided they wanted to be the
boss of Israel, so they came in with their impressive army and forced Israel
to obey them. The Israelites had to pay taxes and obey Roman laws, and
even worship the king of Rome. And if they didn't? They'd be punished, usually through death on a cross. (Many Jewish people were crucified by the
Romans, not just Jesus.)

One day, a Roman centurion (the leader of a group of one hundred soldiers) needed Jesus. His favorite slave was dying. He didn't dare come to
Jesus himself. After all, he was the enemy. Instead, he sent some of his Jewish
friends to beg Jesus to come.

"If anyone deserves your help, he does," they said, "for he loves the Jewish
people and even built a synagogue for us" (Luke 7:4–5).

Jesus could have said no. I don't think anyone would have been angry if
he chose not to help this Roman because, frankly, the Jewish people hated
the Romans and wanted them out of Israel. Jesus probably also knew that
someday he was going to be killed by Romans.

But Jesus's compassion and kindness were for everyone, not just his friends. So he went and healed the Roman centurion's slave. I think Jesus did it for two reasons. First, because Jesus has compassion for defenseless people, and a slave was barely considered human. But he also did it out of compassion for the Roman, who truly loved his slave. Jesus showed us what it looks like to do good to your enemies.

I said before that it's impossible to be kind to an enemy, but that's not quite true. It's impossible to be kind to an enemy *without* God working in your heart. But with God, all things are possible, including being kind to enemies.

Luke 6:35 says that when we show God's kindness to our enemies, we are acting like God, because he is kind to everyone, even those who are unthankful and wicked.

DISCUSSION STARTER
- Tell about a time you felt like someone was your enemy.
- Is there an enemy you could show kindness to this week? How?

PRAYER
Jesus, thank you for showing us what it looks like to choose kindness even when it's hard. Please give us the courage to be kind, even to our enemies. Amen.

DAY 58

REPENTANCE THROUGH KINDNESS

Don't you see how wonderfully kind, tolerant, and patient God is
with you? Does this mean nothing to you? Can't you see that his
kindness is intended to turn you from your sin?

(ROMANS 2:4)

When you do something wrong, what is the best way to get you to apologize
and actually mean it? If I yelled, "You're an awful person," would that make
you apologize? Maybe, but you would only do it because you were scared of
me. What if I said, "If you say you're sorry, I'll give you a cookie!" You might
apologize, but you wouldn't really mean it. You'd just be saying "I'm sorry"
in order to get a cookie. Your heart wouldn't be any different.

Many people think God is exactly like that. They think he is angry with
them, ready to throw lightning bolts at them for being bad. That image actually comes from Zeus, an ancient Greek false god. The real God is definitely
not a lightning bolt thrower. If people don't picture God as an angry guy in
the sky, sometimes they imagine God wants to bribe them into behaving
well. They say, "You give me a bike for Christmas, and I promise to stop
bugging my brother." That idea also comes from ancient times, when people
believed they needed to bring certain sacrifices and gifts to the temples so the
gods would make it rain (or give bikes for Christmas).

When Jesus was dying on the cross, two criminals were crucified right
next to him. One of them made fun of Jesus, just like almost everyone else in
the crowd.

"But the other criminal rebuked him. 'Don't you fear God,' he said, 'since
you are under the same sentence? We are punished justly, for we are getting what our deeds deserve. But this man has done nothing wrong'" (Luke
23:40–41 NIV).

How did the criminal know Jesus was innocent? Maybe he could tell Jesus was different just by watching how he behaved on the cross. Jesus didn't yell at or lecture the people hurling insults at him. He didn't promise punishments for those who crucified him or rewards for those who followed him. He was clearly different. The kindness of Jesus led the criminal to want to stay with him.

Jesus showed kindness by forgiving him, and he shows you kindness too. But remember, God doesn't give you kindness so you can keep it all to yourself! Imagine that I gave you a big bucket full of your favorite cookies, and there were a bunch of other kids around. Do you think I meant for you to keep all those cookies to yourself? No way! By giving you all those cookies, I expected you to share them with others. I'm not going to take them away if you don't share them, or bribe you with another bucket of cookies if you do share. I hope you'll share simply because you know there's enough to go around.

In the same way, God gives you so much kindness, and he hopes you'll share. He won't force you to share his kindness by threatening you with lightning bolts or by bribing you with treats. Instead, God keeps showering his love and kindness on you, so you're so filled up with it that you'll naturally want to pass it on.

DISCUSSION STARTER

- How has God shown kindness to you?
- How can we share God's kindness with each other this week?

PRAYER

Thank you, Jesus, for using kindness, not anger or punishments, to turn us from sin. Please help us show that kind of kindness to others. Amen.

DAY 59

KINDNESS THROUGH PAIN

When Jesus saw his mother standing there beside the disciple he loved, he said to her, "Dear woman, here is your son." And he said to this disciple, "Here is your mother."
(JOHN 19:26–27)

We all have a Worst Day Ever now and then, and usually we try to fix it by doing something for ourselves. What's your favorite way to cheer up on a bad day? Do you like to snuggle on the couch? Do you like to go outside and run as fast as you can, kick a ball, listen to music, or eat cheese? I bet you don't rush out to make a card for your mom, or collect money for the homeless, or write a song for a friend. How do I know that? Because I'm human too, and we rarely think of doing something for other people when we feel crummy.

Jesus had a Worst Day Ever too. It was the day he was nailed to a cross. He didn't try to fix it by doing something for himself, like jumping off the cross and snuggling on the couch, or running away, or listening to music, or eating cheese.

Instead, he looked at his mother, Mary. He knew that Mary was having a Worst Day Ever too. Back when Jesus was still a bitty baby in her arms, a prophet had told her, "This child is destined to cause many in Israel to fall, and many others to rise. . . . And a sword will pierce your very soul" (Luke 2:34–35).

This Worst Day Ever was the day the sword pierced her soul, because she had to watch her oldest son slowly die a horrific death while others laughed at him and tossed dice for his clothes.

But even on this Worst Day Ever, Jesus felt gut-wrenching compassion. This time it was for his mother. And we know what Jesus did when he felt gut-wrenching compassion: he did something to fix it. Jesus couldn't fix Mary's pierced soul and broken heart, but he could make sure that someone would care for his mother. In between pain-filled breaths, Jesus told John and Mary to care for each other like family. Jesus always oozed kindness, even from the cross.

Can I tell you something amazing about kindness? It tends to bounce back. Imagine kindness is like a ball. When you throw a ball to a friend, your friend throws it back. The same thing happens with kindness. When you are kind to someone, some of that kindness will bounce back on you. Knowing you helped someone can make you feel a bit better. It's not easy being kind when you're having a horrible day, even if you're Jesus. It's only through the power of the Holy Spirit that you can show kindness to your sibling or friend or the kid down the street when you're having a bad day. But Jesus shows us that when we have God's help, it really is possible.

DISCUSSION STARTER
- Tell about your own Worst Day Ever (or just a bad day).
- If you can, tell about a time when someone else was having a bad day and yet they still showed kindness to you.

PRAYER
Jesus, thank you for the gift of your kindness even on our worst days. Please help us to keep our eyes open for what you are doing, and may we be kindness bringers to others even when we're having a bad day. Amen.

DAY 60

FAMILIAR KINDNESS

At dawn Jesus was standing on the beach, but the disciples
couldn't see who he was. He called out, "Fellows, have you
caught any fish?"
(JOHN 21:4–5)

In a famous story called *The Magician's Nephew* by C. S. Lewis, the lives of two
children are disrupted when they get tricked into going into another world.
The only person still alive in this other world is an evil queen, and when
they go back home, they accidentally bring her back with them! Everything
has gone wrong, but they try to pretend it never happened and go back to
their old, familiar lives. Eventually they realize how much life has actually
changed because there's now an evil queen tromping around their city, so
they join the adventure again and finally manage to get rid of her.

This is just like what happened to Peter. One morning, Peter's life was
disrupted in a huge way. He had fished all night without a single bite when
a random guy told him to throw his nets on the other side of the boat. Peter
obeyed, and his boat nearly tipped over from the huge catch of fish flopping
in the nets! Of course, we know that random guy was Jesus.

From then on, Peter followed Jesus and became one of his very best
friends. He made a lot of mistakes on the way, but he promised never to leave
Jesus. Then it all went wrong. Jesus was arrested, and Peter was confused
and scared. When asked if they were friends, Peter pretended not to know
Jesus . . . three times!

When Peter realized what he had done, he cried. His best friend was crucified, and Peter thought all was lost.

Then some of Jesus's female disciples came rushing back with a story of
angels and Jesus, risen from the dead. Peter raced to the tomb only to find
empty graveclothes.

Jesus visited the disciples a couple times, but Peter still felt lost. So he did the same thing the children in *The Magician's Nephew* did. He went back to his old, familiar life.

"I'm going out to fish," he said, and several other disciples joined him. But just like that awful night a few years earlier, they caught nothing. Nothing, that is, until Jesus showed up and filled their nets with fish once more.

Jesus didn't need to come back to the disciples. He could have ditched them and looked for new friends. But instead, he showed incredible kindness by filling their nets with fish even though they had deserted him. He showed kindness by feeding them breakfast and calling them to share his story with others. He gave them another chance to join the adventure.

Someday you might meet someone who doesn't want to follow Jesus anymore. When you do, remember that Jesus always gives them another chance to join the adventure. Your job is just to remind them of Jesus's kindness.

DISCUSSION STARTER

- How has God shown you his love and kindness?
- Do you know someone who turned away from God or pretended they weren't a Christian? How can you show God's kindness to them?

PRAYER

Thank you, Jesus, for your kindness which brings us to repentance. Take the truths we have learned and plant them deep in our hearts so they grow the fruit of kindness in our lives. Amen.

GOODNESS

HANDS-ON GROWTH ACTIVITIES

Use these activities as a hands-on supplement to the daily devotions. You can add in one per day, flip to this page for an idea only on days when you have a few extra minutes, or use a few of the activities each Sunday.

Memorize it: Memorize Galatians 6:9 together over the next two weeks.

Write it: Write Galatians 6:9 in fancy letters. Hang it on your wall.

Draw it: Draw a picture of some of the gifts God has given you.

Pray it: Pray a breath prayer. As you breathe in, say, "How great is the goodness . . ." and as you breathe out, say, "you have stored up for me."

Research it: Use an online Bible to search for the word "gift" in the New Testament. What do you notice?

Imagine it: Close your eyes and think back to the worst thing you've ever done. Now imagine Jesus standing beside you. What does he do with your sin?

Play it: Plan a "secret friend" day in your family. Each family member should choose someone else's name. Pick a due date, and have each person create a good gift to share with their secret friend.

Sing it: Sing a song of God's goodness! If you can't think of one, make one up.

Ask it: What would be different if our God wasn't a good God?

Speak it: Pretend you are a farmer. Act like you are moving rocks, making rows, planting seed, watering, and weeding. Then speak Galatians 6:9 out loud.

For Bible verse printables and other activities,
please visit fruitofthespiritbook.com.

DAY 61

GOOD GOD

As Jesus was starting out on his way to Jerusalem, a man came
running up to him, knelt down, and asked, "Good Teacher,
what must I do to inherit eternal life?"
"Why do you call me good?" Jesus asked.
"Only God is truly good."
(MARK 10:17–18)

What is "goodness" all about? What does it mean to "be good"? If I say *please*
and *thank you* to my mom, is that enough? Am I a good person if I try to help
others? Does God think I'm a good person?

Wow, that's a lot of questions. I guess being good is more complicated than
we thought!

To learn about goodness, let's do what we've been doing this whole book:
let's look at Jesus. What does he say about goodness?

Once, a man came running up to Jesus, knelt down, called him "Good
Teacher," then asked a big, complicated question. He called Jesus "Good
Teacher" just to be polite, but Jesus called him out on it because goodness is
more than being a smart person or a good teacher.

Only God is truly good. To say that God is good means that he *always* does
what is right. There is nothing bad or evil or dark about God, so he always
chooses to do the right thing. He is *good*—all the time.

Can you imagine being good all the time? That means never lying, even a
little bit. It means never saying something mean, or taking a cookie without
permission, or yelling at your mom, or feeling sorry for yourself. Wow, that
would be hard.

It is hard. In fact, it's impossible to be truly good. That's why Jesus said that
"only God is good." But Jesus *is* God, so when we look at Jesus's life, we see
the only human being who was ever truly good. Jesus was good even when

no one was looking. He was good when people tried to kill him, when his friends turned away from him, and even when he was flipping over tables in the temple.

That brings us to a problem. If only God is good, then how can you and I grow in the fruit of goodness? Can we ever be good?

Goodness starts by accepting that God forgave your sin through Jesus's death on the cross. Then, it continues as the Holy Spirit works inside you to make you more like Jesus. He helps you practice doing the right thing even when no one is looking, when life is hard, and even if your friends turn away because you follow Jesus.

DISCUSSION STARTER

- When is it hard for you to be good?
- How do you think Jesus would act in that situation?

PRAYER

Jesus, thank you for being a perfect example of goodness and for sending your Spirit to help us grow in goodness too. Help us to practice goodness so we can show others how good you are. Amen.

DAY 62

GOOD GIFTS

"If you sinful people know how to give good gifts to your
children, how much more will your heavenly Father
give good gifts to those who ask him."
(MATTHEW 7:11)

What's the worst gift you've ever received? I've gotten a few doozies, but
the one I'll remember forever is the gift my parents gave me the Christmas
I was seventeen. We snuggled on the couch in our PJs, snacking on tangy
Christmas orange slices and sticky-sweet candy canes. My younger sister
opened her gift first, and she squealed with delight. She ripped open the box
and pulled out a camera, holding it in front of her face like she was going to
take a snapshot of my bedhead and PJs.

I secretly hoped I'd get a camera too, but when I opened my gift, I scowled.
It was a big, ugly, puke-green suitcase. I wanted to shout, "Bah, humbug!" but
instead I said a polite thank-you and sat back down. Were my parents trying
to get rid of me? Did they want me to move away? And why on earth would
they choose the most disgusting color in the world? Ugh.

But it turns out that my ugly green suitcase was a better gift than I originally thought. I used it to bring my clothes to college and to travel to several
other countries in the world. Because it was so ugly, I didn't have any trouble
with anyone trying to steal it. Even though I didn't like my ugly green suitcase at first, it turned out to be a really good gift after all.

One time, Jesus was trying to explain God's goodness, and he used the
example of a parent giving good gifts to their child.

He said, "You parents—if your children ask for a loaf of bread, do you give
them a stone instead? Or if they ask for a fish, do you give them a snake? Of
course not!" (Matthew 7:9–10).

Good parents don't give mean gifts to their children. Parents give gifts to their children because they love them and want the best for them, and so does God.

Sometimes God's gifts are obviously good, like seeing a sudden rainbow in the middle of a gloomy day or finding a friendly ladybug under a leaf. But other times it takes a little more time to see the goodness in God's gift. Maybe you didn't get to be in class with your best friend this year, or you got a different teacher or Sunday school leader than the one you really wanted. Or maybe you had to move to a new city. Those might not feel like good gifts, but if you put on some imaginary "goodness glasses," you can see God's goodness shining through almost every situation.

Sometimes we don't notice a good gift because we don't understand how it will help us, like my suitcase. But God's gifts are always good.

DISCUSSION STARTER
- What good gifts has God given to you?
- Think of a gift you received (from a person or God) that didn't seem good at first but turned out good in the end. What was it?
- What's one good gift we can give this week to show someone else God's goodness?

PRAYER
God, you are a good Father who gives good gifts to us. Thank you for showing us what goodness truly is, and please help us to show that goodness to others. Amen.

DAY 63

TROUBLESOME GOODNESS

He answered, "If you had a sheep that fell into a well on the
Sabbath, wouldn't you work to pull it out? Of course you would.
And how much more valuable is a person than a sheep! Yes, the
law permits a person to do good on the Sabbath."
(MATTHEW 12:11–12)

Have you ever gotten in trouble for being good? That seems a little strange, doesn't it? Who gets in trouble for being good? But sometimes our world is so twisted that people think doing good is the wrong thing.

During the Second World War, people everywhere started doing horrible things to Jewish people. In many parts of Europe, the government forced Jews to leave their homes and march to camps where they were murdered. You would think people would realize how awful this was, but most people, including a lot of Christians, pretended it was okay. Six million Jewish men, women, and children were killed. Even in places where Jews weren't being rounded up and killed, people didn't want them around. Most countries refused to let Jews come in, even though they were running for their lives.

In the midst of this evil, some families chose to do what was good. For example, the family of Corrie ten Boom built a tiny secret room in their house to hide Jews in. It was just big enough for six people, and when the soldiers came, they had to stand still and be perfectly quiet. Because of their safe house and a few others the ten Booms helped start, they saved eight hundred Jews. But what they did was against the law, and eventually someone tattled on them. The entire ten Boom family was sent to the death camps, and only Corrie survived. They got in trouble for doing good.

Jesus got in trouble for doing good too. Once, he went to a synagogue on the Sabbath. One of the Ten Commandments is all about not doing any work on the Sabbath day. It was just for worshipping God. But when Jesus got to the synagogue, he saw a man with a shriveled hand. The leaders tried to trick him by asking, "Does the law permit a person to work by healing on the Sabbath?" (Matthew 12:10).

Jesus is pretty good at not getting tricked, though, so he reminded them that God wants us to do good all the time. Doing good is never against God's laws. So he healed the man, and the Pharisees set up a meeting to decide how to get rid of Jesus. Jesus definitely got in trouble for doing good.

There might be times when you have to decide between doing what is good and following the rules. Let's imagine that your Sunday school teacher has a rule about tattling. Normally adults make rules like this because a tattletale just wants to get another kid in trouble. But what if some of the kids are being really mean to the new kid, and the teacher doesn't notice? Do you break the rule by tattling, or do you keep the rule? The good thing would be to break the rule and tell the teacher, even if you might get in trouble. God will help you do the right thing.

DISCUSSION STARTER

- Let's think of an example of how someone might get in trouble for doing the right thing.

PRAYER

God, please help us to be brave like you, to choose to do what is good and right even if we might get into trouble. Amen.

DAY 64

NEIGHBORLY GOODNESS

"Now which of these three would you say was a neighbor to the
man who was attacked by bandits?" Jesus asked.
The man replied, "The one who showed him mercy."
Then Jesus said, "Yes, now go and do the same."
(LUKE 10:36–37)

Imagine that you are setting out on a journey through the wilderness. You fill
the pack of your favorite donkey with water and snacks, tuck some money
in your pocket, and set out. It's kind of like the setup for one of those old
Western movies.

The going is good at first. Rocks crunch underfoot, and the air smells fresh.
But eventually you must walk down into a canyon. The shadows deepen, and
strange shuffling noises make you stop. Small, dark caves line the walls of the
canyon. You grasp the donkey's rope with both hands, then move forward
cautiously. Your mouth feels dry and sticky, but you need to keep moving.

Suddenly you see something lying on the side of the road. Your donkey
brays loudly. Is it a trick? Sometimes bandits pretend to be injured; then
when a traveler stops, they jump on you and steal everything. You tiptoe
closer to get a better look. Whoever it is, it looks like the bandits already got
to him. His clothes are torn, he's all beat up, and he's not even wearing shoes
anymore. He is breathing, though, so he's still alive.

You chew your lip. This man is clearly from your enemy's hometown. If
he met you on the road, he'd probably spit at you or climb into a tree to avoid
you. Your people and his people have hated each other for hundreds of years.

But even though he's your enemy, he needs help. You pour some antiseptic
on his cuts to clean them, then bandage him up. You gently lay him on your
donkey and take him to an inn, where he'll be safe. You have to continue on
your trip, but you don't want to just leave him there alone. Instead, you give

the innkeeper some of the few coins you have left so she'll care for him until you can come back.

Have you ever heard this story before? It's a story Jesus told. We call it "the parable of the Good Samaritan." Being good means doing the right thing even when it's hard, which is exactly what the Samaritan did. He didn't earn any awards for helping the wounded man. He did it because it was the right thing to do.

It's not always going to be easy to do the right thing, especially to people you don't like. Sometimes you're going to mess it up. Only Jesus did the right thing all the time. But Jesus sends you his Spirit to help you do the right thing, all the time, even to people who feel like enemies.

DISCUSSION STARTER

- What makes the "Good Samaritan" good?
- Is Jesus asking you to do something good for someone today?

PRAYER

Jesus, thank you for this reminder of what true goodness looks like. Please help us notice when those around us need help, and give us the courage to show your goodness to them, even if it's someone we don't like. Amen.

DAY 65

TOUGH GOODNESS

Jesus called his disciples to him and said, "I tell you the truth,
this poor widow has given more than all the others who are
making contributions. For they gave a tiny part of their surplus,
but she, poor as she is, has given everything she had to live on."
(MARK 12:43–44)

Do you find it fairly easy to be a good person? Do you easily think of ways to help your siblings, or are you constantly fighting with them? Is it easy for you to give gifts to others or money to those in need, or is it really hard to share like that? Some people find it hard to be good and kind and loving, and some people don't, which is why I want to point you to an odd little conversation Jesus had with his disciples.

People often came to the temple to give money, which was used by priests to take care of the beautiful building. One day, Jesus watched as people gave their offerings. Many rich people walked in, coins clanking like marbles in a jar. Their offerings were impressive. Surely God must love the amazing gifts they were giving to him!

Then a poor widow came by. Her husband had died, and women in those days didn't often get jobs. The only thing she had left in the world was two copper coins; they were practically worthless. Jesus watched her put them quietly in the box.

He was so impressed with her tiny little offering that he called his disciples over to tell them how amazing it was. It must have surprised them that her teeny tiny offering was better than the heavy bags of coins the rich men had brought.

Here's why he was so impressed: the people who brought the heavy bags of coins had lots of money still at home. Their offerings weren't bad, but they didn't show true goodness. It was easy for them to give. The widow's offering showed true goodness because she was willing to give everything to God. Can you imagine how hard that was?

If you find it easy to be good, that's wonderful. You're like the rich men who gave bags of coins. Those coins would be used to serve God but weren't a big sacrifice for the givers.

Sometimes it can feel like we don't have very much goodness inside us. If you find it hard to be good, like you're always getting into trouble or it's super hard to remember to share or give to others, remember that God loves and accepts you. God's goodness isn't about being the nicest person around, and being good isn't a contest with God. No one is perfect in God's eyes, even the kid who always knows the right answer and helps pass out the worksheets. The important thing is that God is slowly changing your heart, helping you want to become more good.

And hey, if you are the kid who always knows the right answers and helps pass out the worksheets, remember that God wants to use you to encourage your friends toward goodness, not make them feel bad when they make a mistake.

DISCUSSION STARTER

- When do you find it easy to be good?
- How could you ask for Jesus's help at a time when it's hard to be good?

PRAYER

Jesus, thank you that being good isn't a contest. Help us to choose goodness even when it's hard and to encourage others when they're struggling to make good choices. Amen.

DAY 66

PRETEND GOODNESS

"You have heard that our ancestors were told, 'You must not murder. If you commit murder, you are subject to judgment.' But I say, if you are even angry with someone, you are subject to judgment! If you call someone an idiot, you are in danger of being brought before the court. And if you curse someone, you are in danger of the fires of hell."
(MATTHEW 5:21–22)

Have you ever tried a food that looked really good on the outside but then was really disgusting on the inside? My kids sometimes like to buy those jelly beans that look like regular, tasty jelly beans. The jelly beans are a mean trick, though, because half of the candies tastes great, and the other half actually tastes like boogers or vomit. Yuck!

Sometimes humans can be like that too. We can look really good on the outside, like a juicy, pear-flavored jelly bean, when we're really gross on the inside, like musty toenail clippings. I don't mean that we're literally filled with toenail clippings (thank goodness), but that our hearts can get filled up with gunk.

When God looks at you and me, he doesn't just look at what's on the outside. You can put on all the clean clothes and hair gel you want, but God can see right through that into your mind and heart. He can see you plotting revenge while sitting in Sunday school, or poking your sister while singing songs at church. He knows when you look at the new kid and judge him based on how he walks, and he knows you hate the annoying girl down the street.

Here's the thing about true goodness: it's not *just* about what we do. It's about who we are when no one else is looking. In the verses we just read, Jesus said that when we call someone an idiot or get angry at them, it comes from the same dark place in our hearts that would cause a person to murder someone. Yikes! That's because God knows how easy it is for us to pretend to be good. We can do all the right things, but if we do them while angry or disrespectful or whiny, it's not true goodness.

King David knew all about pretend goodness. He took someone else's wife and tried to pretend it was OK. But God knew what was in his heart. David wrote this song to God as part of his apology:

> Create in me a clean heart, O God.
> Renew a loyal spirit within me. (Psalm 51:10)

God can clean our hearts too, so we are just as good inside as we look on the outside. All you have to do is ask.

DISCUSSION STARTER

- Share something that you do in your mind but don't usually talk about. (Maybe you judge people, think mean thoughts, make revenge plans, or hate someone.)

PRAYER

God, we're sorry for the times we've pretended to be good while having all kinds of bad thoughts. The next time our hearts are full of trash, please remind us to let you create clean hearts in us. Amen.

DAY 67

NO JUDGMENT

"Do not judge others, and you will not be judged."
(MATTHEW 7:1)

Imagine that you wake up with a pounding headache. Your left eyeball feels like someone is pushing a fork through it. You take a warm shower and a pain killer, and it seems to go away. When you get to the breakfast table, your mom gives you a weird look. "Is everything OK, honey?" she asks as she plops pancakes on your plate. You stare at her. Is it just you, or is it hard to blink your left eye? But the pain is gone so you just nod and shovel pancakes into your face.

All morning, you randomly get pain in your left eyeball, and everyone you meet gives you weird looks. Then you meet someone with a bigger problem than weird looks and random pain. A kid you know is walking around with a big red spot in her eye! Ew, so gross.

"Let me help you get rid of that spot," you say. But when you lean in, it feels like that fork is stabbing your eyeball again. A kid behind you starts laughing.

"Look! That kid with a huge log in the eye is trying to help the girl with the little red spot in *her* eye!"

What? You have a log in your eye? You rush to the bathroom to look in the mirror. How absurd! You've been walking around all day with a huge log sticking out of your left eyeball, and you didn't even know it.

Can you imagine that happening to you? It's pretty funny to think that you could go a whole day without noticing a huge log in your eye, but we do stuff like this all the time. Jesus once said that judging someone is like trying to get a speck out of your friend's eye when you have a log sticking out of your own eye. Judging means to think bad thoughts about someone, especially when you don't know that much about who they are.

For example, you might look at a girl who keeps getting into trouble and think, "That's a bad kid," but you don't know what her life has been like. She might not be able to concentrate on reading because no one knows she needs glasses, or maybe her dog just died. You might behave just like she does if you had the same problems. You aren't a good judge of her life because you have a log in your eye.

Judgmental people are just like the kid with the log in his or her eye. You can be that person, or you can be the kind of person with goodness in your heart, choosing to treat others with grace no matter what.

DISCUSSION STARTER

- What kind of person are you most likely to judge? How can you be kind to them instead?

PRAYER

Thank you, Jesus, for giving us second (and third and fourth) chances! Help us think about and treat other people kindly without judging them so we can give them the same chance you gave us. Amen.

DAY 68

GOLDEN GOODNESS

"Do to others whatever you would like them to do to you."
(MATTHEW 7:12)

Our verse for today is what people call the Golden Rule. About five hundred years before Jesus, a popular teacher named Confucius shared a similar rule. He said, "What you do not want done to yourself, do not do to others." Do you think that's the same rule as the one Jesus said, or different?

According to Confucius's rule, if I don't want to get punched, I shouldn't punch anyone else. That sounds fair, right? But it doesn't say anything about doing anything good for anyone else, just that I shouldn't do something bad.

On the other hand, Jesus's rule teaches us that we ought to treat others well, no matter what. This is a huge part of what "goodness" means: to treat others well, no matter who they are and what they've done.

The night before he died, Jesus gave us an amazing example of doing to others what you would like them to do to you. He was about to have a very special meal with his disciples, and they all came in from the streets of Jerusalem. After walking around all day in sandals, no one wanted someone else's stinky feet next to them at supper, so normally a servant would wash the feet of the guests. But no servant was there to wash the disciples' feet, and none of them volunteered to do it for the others. During the meal, they even argued about who would be the greatest in Jesus's kingdom!

Without a lecture or a wagging finger, Jesus wrapped a towel around his waist, poured water into a little tub, and began to wash his disciples' feet. Jesus even washed the feet of Judas, who would betray him that very evening.

Jesus didn't just teach the Golden Rule. He lived it.

I know that some days it feels impossible to treat others with goodness in your heart. Sometimes people just get on your nerves. Maybe it's a sibling, a parent, or another kid, but there's often someone in our lives who seems intent on driving us crazy.

But here's something to think about: maybe God has put that person in your life so you can practice goodness. No, you won't always get it right. But you can start at the Confucius level by not doing evil, and let the Holy Spirit help you move toward actually doing good to that person. As you practice, the fruit of goodness will grow in your heart so you will be able to live out the Golden Rule too.

DISCUSSION STARTER

- What would happen if all Christians in the world followed the Golden Rule all the time?
- What would happen in our family if we choose to behave like this all the time?

PRAYER

Jesus, thank you for your amazing example of goodness and for giving us the Holy Spirit so we can grow in goodness. Please help us to treat others with kindness and love every day. Amen.

DAY 69

TREASURE-BOX HEART

"A good person produces good things from the treasury of a
good heart, and an evil person produces evil things from the
treasury of an evil heart."
(LUKE 6:45)

Close your eyes for a minute and imagine that inside your chest lies a treasure box. That treasure box is your heart. Every time you speak or move, the
treasure box opens just a crack. When you have Jesus in your heart, you have
his light inside you and your treasure-box heart leaks a little bit of light into
the world. Without Jesus, you have a black hole in that treasure box, which
sucks a little happiness and joy from the room you're in.

Did you know that others can tell what's in your treasure box based on
how you talk and live your life? Jesus said that someone with a good heart
will do and say good things, and someone with an evil heart will do and
say evil things. When we become Christians, we have Jesus's light inside us,
but we don't immediately become perfectly good. We still have black-hole
moments, times when the dark places in our hearts leak out. We have to
let Jesus work in our hearts so he can keep filling those dark spots with his
light.

Jesus showed what his treasure-box heart held when he was arrested.
When Jesus's disciples saw him betrayed and about to be arrested, they
panicked. One of them whipped out a sword and slashed off a servant's ear!
Jesus could have dashed away in the confusion or at least given his disciple
a thumbs-up for defending him. Instead, he lifted his hand to the man's ear
and healed him, proving that his treasure-box heart was completely overflowing with light and goodness.

Jesus was the only person who ever lived whose heart was completely
like a bright star. In fact, in Revelation 22:16, Jesus calls himself the bright

morning star. Every time he spoke or moved or looked at someone, his trea-sure-box heart leaked goodness and joy and peace into the world. When he died, it seemed that the darkness had won. But he rose again.

Even though you and I still have black-hole moments, we know that Jesus's light inside us will keep getting brighter as we keep spending time with him. His Spirit living inside us will keep helping us grow in goodness. All we have to do is ask that he help us open our treasure box a little wider.

DISCUSSION STARTER

- If someone looked at your life, would they guess that you have Jesus's light in your heart? Why or why not?
- Our hearts can tend to be more like a black hole even when we have Jesus living there. What could you do when you have black-hole moments?

PRAYER

Jesus, thank you for the goodness inside you that changed the whole world. Please fill our hearts with your goodness and light, and help us live in ways that show your goodness to the world. Amen.

DAY 70

SUPER GOODNESS

By his divine power, God has given us everything we need for
living a godly life.
(2 PETER 1:3)

If you could have a superpower, what would it be? I think I'd like to be able
to summon fire, because then I'd never be cold!

This verse in 2 Peter tells us about a different kind of power—the power to
live a godly life. Maybe that doesn't seem as exciting as having the power to fly
or turn invisible or lift up an elephant with your pinky finger, but it's a superpower that can change the world. People who live godly lives have stopped
slavery, changed unfair laws, written books and songs that changed hearts,
made inventions and calculations that got humans to the moon, saved lives, and
changed entire countries. Some of those adventures might be in your future as
you follow God, but he can change the world through you even as a kid.

The Bible tells us that God has an infinite store of glory and goodness and
that we have access to it through the Holy Spirit.

After Jesus died on the cross for our sins and then came back to life to beat
the power of sin and death forever, he went back to heaven. He knew that as
a physical, touchable person, he could only be with a few people at a time.
That means he could only help and teach a few people at a time. So instead of
sticking around forever, Jesus went back to heaven and sent his Spirit to live
in the hearts of his followers. That means every Christian everywhere has
God with them all the time.

Having the Holy Spirit in our hearts is the same as having Jesus inside us,
teaching us and giving us power to become more like him. And guess what?
You and I have access to the same Holy Spirit. If you've chosen to follow
Jesus, you don't get a kid-sized portion of the Holy Spirit. You have just as
much as any of those people who lived incredible, godly lives.

In fact, there's a prayer that one of the apostles prayed for every single believer that I'm praying for you too: "So we keep on praying for you, asking our God to enable you to live a life worthy of his call. May he give you the power to accomplish all the good things your faith prompts you to do" (2 Thessalonians 1:11).

May God give you the superpower of living a godly life that changes the world.

DISCUSSION STARTER

- When it's hard to be good, what do you do?
- What is one problem in the world that you would like to solve?

PRAYER

Thank you, God, for being the source of all goodness and for giving us everything we need for a godly life. Please take the truths we have learned and plant them deep in our hearts, so they grow the fruit of goodness in our lives. Amen.

FAITHFULNESS

HANDS-ON GROWTH ACTIVITIES

Use these activities as a hands-on supplement to the daily devotions. You can add in one per day, flip to this page for an idea only on days when you have a few extra minutes, or use a few of the activities each Sunday.

Memorize it: Memorize Lamentations 3:22–23 together over the next two weeks.

Write it: Write Lamentations 3:22–23 in big block letters. Hang it on your wall.

Draw it: Draw a picture of Lamentations 3:22–23 with you in the middle of the picture. What is around you, trying to consume you? What does God's faithfulness look like to you?

Pray it: Pray a breath prayer: As you breathe in, say, "When I am faithless . . ." and as you breathe out, say, "you remain faithful."

Research it: Look up the covenants that God made with Abraham (Genesis 15 and 17) and with David (2 Samuel 7 and 1 Chronicles 17). How long ago were those promises made? Was God faithful to them?

Imagine it: Close your eyes and imagine that someone is threatening to hurt you unless you stop following Jesus. Now imagine Jesus is standing right beside you. How does he help you stand firm?

Play it: Play a game of hide-and-seek. Can you ever hide from God? Will God hide from you?

Sing it: Find (or make up) a song about God's faithfulness.

Ask it: What would be different if our God wasn't a faithful God?

Speak it: Stand up and speak 2 Corinthians 1:21 in your firmest, strongest voice.

For Bible verse printables and other activities,
please visit fruitofthespiritbook.com.

DAY 71

FOLLOWING FAITHFULLY

Think carefully about this Jesus whom we declare to be God's
messenger and High Priest. For he was faithful to God,
who appointed him.
(HEBREWS 3:1–2)

Have you ever seen a farm or garden where the plants were all growing in perfectly straight rows, or a lawn where the stripes from the mower were completely straight? It seems like magic (or at least math) must be involved, but there's a simple trick to making perfectly straight rows.

Imagine you are driving a tractor or lawn mower. Look out into the distance and find a tree that's straight across from you. Then, without taking your eyes off the tree, drive. Never look down; always look at the point in the distance. If you look down, your rows will get wiggly because it's impossible to drive straight while looking down. You also need to make sure you pick something that doesn't move as your guide. Can you imagine what would happen to your rows if you chose to look at a cow instead of a tree?

Driving a straight line on a tractor is kind of like living a life of faithfulness. Let me explain.

The author of Hebrews imagines that living our lives is like running a race. We want to do our very best, so we get rid of everything that slows us down, like sin. And we want to keep running without stopping. Hebrews 12:2 says that "we do this by keeping our eyes on Jesus, the champion who initiates and perfects our faith."

Jesus is like that tree at the end of the field. When we keep our spiritual eyes on him, we can keep running the race faithfully because he is faithful. He is like a steady tree to look at, not like a wandering cow. We can trust Jesus to be our steady, faithful guide because he is faithful himself.

But what is faithfulness, anyway?

Faithfulness is about habits. Someone who is a faithful lover has a habit of loving well. A person who is faithful in joy has a habit of joy. In fact, faithfulness combines all the other fruits of the Spirit. Jesus wasn't sometimes loving, sometimes peaceful, and sometimes joyful. He had a habit of love, peace, and joy, which means he was faithful.

Jesus had a habit of spending time alone with his Father. He had a habit of healing others. He had a habit of seeing the potential in people. All of those things made him someone the disciples could fix their eyes on and follow forever.

He's still worth fixing our eyes on and following forever.

DISCUSSION STARTER

- How can we fix our eyes on Jesus every day, not just when we remember to read this devotional book?

PRAYER

Thank you, Jesus, for being faithful and for being a faithful guide we can follow through life. You won't ever let us down. Please give us the strength and desire to fix our eyes on you every day. Amen.

DAY 72

MISSION FAITHFUL

"Didn't you know that I must be in my Father's house?"
(LUKE 2:49)

Once when he was a kid, Jesus got separated from his parents while they were visiting the big city of Jerusalem. He was from the small town of Nazareth, but they took the sixty-mile trek to Jerusalem once per year to celebrate a festival called the Passover. On the way home, Mary assumed Jesus was with the men, and Joseph assumed Jesus was with the women and children. But he wasn't with either, so Mary and Joseph rushed back to Jerusalem, frantic to find their son.

They eventually found him sitting in the temple with the teachers and religious leaders. He had been listening to the leaders, asking questions and even giving some answers too. They were astounded at his understanding.

Of course, Mary and Joseph were a little bit ticked off. They'd been frantically searching for him for days, and here he was, happily chatting with the religious teachers. That would be like your mom searching for hours for you, only to find you under the table, happily eating ice cream.

But Jesus said something strange: "Didn't you know that I must be in my Father's house?" (Luke 2:49). Even at age twelve, Jesus knew what he was supposed to be doing, and he did it. He knew that part of his mission here on earth was to help others really understand who God is, so he went to the temple to discuss God with the teachers there.

I'm going to teach you another Greek word, but don't worry, this one is easy! It's the word *dei*, and it means "must." This same Greek word was used for other things that Jesus said he absolutely *must* do.

Jesus said he *must* suffer many terrible things and be rejected (Mark 8:31); he *must* preach the Good News of the Kingdom of God (Luke 4:43); he *must* be lifted up (John 3:14); he *must* rise from the dead on the third day (Luke 24:46);

as the Good Shepherd, he *must* bring all his sheep together into one fold (John 10:16); and he *must* do what God had sent him to do (John 9:4).

Jesus knew what God had called him to do, and he was faithful to carry out his mission. Sometimes we find it hard to carry out God's mission to become more like him and to share him with others, but the Holy Spirit can grow the fruit of faithfulness in our lives.

DISCUSSION STARTER

- Jesus knew what his mission was, but we don't always know what God wants us to do. Read Romans 12:2. How do you get to know what God's mission is for you?

PRAYER

Thank you, Jesus, for being faithful to the Father's mission. Please transform us to be more like you so we can know what your mission is for us, and help us to be faithful to carry it out. Amen.

DAY 73

FAITHFUL PRAYER

Before daybreak the next morning, Jesus got up and went out to
an isolated place to pray.
(MARK 1:35)

Have you ever gone for a hike and found a bubbling brook, dancing and rippling past your feet? Maybe you reached down and took a sip or slipped off your shoes and soaked your toes in the refreshingly cool water. But if you went back to that brook in the hottest, driest part of the summer, you might discover that something happened to it. There might be just a trickle of water slip-sliding past, or it might even be completely dried up. (Oh dear, your feet will have to stay sweating in their stinky socks.)

Why is that? In the driest part of the summer, there isn't very much rain. There isn't much water going into the brook, so there is very little water for drinking or cooling off.

The same thing can happen in our spiritual lives. We might go to church and feel really close to God for an hour, but then we go home and forget to connect with him all week. If our hearts are like a brook, and if we're only getting God's rain once per week, that isn't enough to keep us filled up. If we're not filled up with God's rain of love and peace, it's hard for us to share them with others.

Jesus knew this could happen to him too. He was constantly slipping off to a quiet place to pray. His disciples didn't understand it. They'd wake up and he'd be gone, then they'd search for him and give him a mini lecture when they found him. "Uh, hello! Everyone is looking for you! What are you doing out here by yourself?"

Jesus snuck off to pray so he was constantly being filled up with the Father's love and joy. He was like a brook that was receiving constant rain so he could continue to be a place of healing, refreshing, and love for others.

At this particular time, after Jesus prayed, he knew exactly where he was supposed to go next and why he was supposed to go there. Being faithful in prayer helped him be faithful to follow God's mission for him.

God loves for us to pray any time, and he doesn't get angry if you're not faithful in prayer. But he's always there waiting for us to talk with him. When we learn to become faithful in prayer, we also become like refreshing brooks that offer comfort and love for others.

DISCUSSION STARTER

- Do you have a habit of prayer? If so, when do you pray?
- How can our family build a stronger prayer habit, so we're constantly being filled with God's Spirit of love, joy, and peace?

PRAYER

Jesus, thank you for modeling this habit of prayer. Please make us thirsty for more of you so we remember to come to you in prayer every day. Amen.

DAY 74

STANDING FIRM

It is God who enables us, along with you, to stand firm for Christ.
(2 CORINTHIANS 1:21)

Once, I was in a beach town when a storm whipped up. Trees bent nearly sideways and the wind picked up sand and hurled it at my face, my legs, my arms . . . it stung like a thousand tiny bug bites all at once. Waves sloshed like a bowl full of soup as the wind swirled and churned. My family ran for cover.

Hurricanes, sandstorms, or even just a solidly windy day can push us around and even hurt us. Sometimes life is like that too. There are days when it seems like everything goes wrong and the winds of life are trying to hurtle us off a ledge. That would be great if we were hang gliding, but no one likes to get pushed around by life. Sometimes you find out that none of your friends are on your sports team, or you have to move to a new town. Or maybe your mom and dad aren't getting along, or someone makes fun of you for being a Christian. When these things happen, we want to just climb into bed and hide under the covers (or yell at someone) until things get better again.

Faithfulness can be described as standing firm. But how can we stand firm when life is behaving like a storm that wants to blow us off our feet and leave us flat on our backs?

The verse we just read reminds us of something true about faithfulness. It says that God enables us to stand firm for Christ.

Think of it this way. Imagine you are trying to stand waist-deep in the ocean. The top of you is getting blasted with wind, and the bottom of you is getting pushed around by constant, swirling waves. There's only squishy sand beneath your feet, no firm footing. Your knees will start to buckle soon, because no one can stay upright in those conditions. But now imagine that Jesus stands in front of you and wraps you in a huge hug. He is strong and sturdy and doesn't need firm footing because he can stand right on the waves. Now, no matter how windy or wavy it gets, you can stand firm, safe in Jesus's arms.

Jesus helps you stand firm in your faith and love and truth and joy and peace. Even if someone laughs at you or hurts you for following Jesus, or if bad things happen in your life, Jesus will always be there, wrapping his arms around you in a big hug.

DISCUSSION STARTER

- Tell about a time in your life that felt really hard.
- Let's close our eyes and imagine Jesus hugging us right now. How does it feel?

PRAYER

Thank you, God, for making us stand firm in Christ. Help us remember that you are the one who makes us faithful. Amen.

DAY 75

CONSTANT GROWTH

Jesus also said, "The Kingdom of God is like a farmer who
scatters seed on the ground. Night and day, while he's asleep or
awake, the seed sprouts and grows, but he does not understand
how it happens. The earth produces the crops on its own. First a
leaf blade pushes through, then the heads of wheat are formed,
and finally the grain ripens. And as soon as the grain is ready,
the farmer comes and harvests it with a sickle,
for the harvest time has come."
(MARK 4:26–29)

Imagine you're on a farm in the springtime. You create long rows in the soil
and tuck seeds inside, covering them up with dirt as you step from row to
row.

A couple weeks later, the first sprout lifts its leaves above the soil. Wow!
You quickly paint a little wooden sign and pound it into the ground. The
sign says, "First Seedling Up." Two days later, all the seedlings are above
the soil and you go out with another sign, this time attached to a measuring
stick. This sign says, "First Plant That's One Foot Tall Wins a Trophy." You
go out to your plants every day to read books and sing to them to make
sure they grow big and strong. Some days you even bring pom-poms and do
some cheers to make sure they feel good about themselves. As each seedling
gets its third pair of leaves, you type up a report card so it knows that it's
doing a good job.

That's a little silly, isn't it? It's silly because none of those things actually
affect plant growth. Plants don't need awards or cheers or contests in order
to grow. They just grow. That's another picture of what faithfulness is like.

Faithfulness is like a plant that keeps growing through the night and
day. We may not completely understand it, but the plant just keeps doing its

thing every day and every night, and it keeps growing, eventually producing grain, fruit, vegetables, or nuts.

Some plants grow quick; millet grows from a tiny seed to produce grain you can eat for breakfast in just thirty days. Other plants grow slow; some cherry trees can take seven years before you see a single juicy cherry. Different speeds of growth are just fine, because God made all plants well.

In the same way, it might feel like it's taking you forever to grow certain fruits of the Spirit while your little sister already has them all figured out. But God doesn't ask you to be like your little sister. He simply wants you to be faithful to keep following him. As you faithfully follow God each day, as best you can, he does the hardest work of changing you to be more like Jesus.

DISCUSSION STARTER

- Let's imagine your heart is a plant. In what ways are its roots going deep into God's love? How is it getting watered by God's truth? When do you let God's faithful light shine on it?

PRAYER

Thank you, God, for this image of a plant faithfully growing. Please help us to faithfully follow you each day. Amen.

DAY 76

CONSTANT SALTINESS

"You are the salt of the earth. But what good is salt if it has lost
its flavor? Can you make it salty again? It will be thrown out and
trampled underfoot as worthless."
(MATTHEW 5:13)

If I placed a plate of cooked veggies in front of you, what would you reach
for? Ketchup? Hot sauce? Your dog? The easiest thing to grab is the seasoning
that's been around for thousands of years: salt.

Why do we love salt so much? Salt doesn't have its own flavor, but when we
put it on our food, our brains are able to detect flavors that are already in the
food. Salt doesn't change the taste, but it makes food better by bringing out
flavors that are already there. That's why you can add salt to bread and cake
and vegetables and they don't taste salty. They just taste like better bread,
better cake, and better vegetables. In fact, if you have two identical bowls of
chocolate pudding, the one with salt will taste sweeter. That's because when
salt dissolves, one part of it (the sodium) suppresses the bitter flavors, which
makes food sweeter. You don't need a lot of salt to make something better;
just a sprinkle is enough to make a whole meal taste delicious.

Jesus compared his followers to salt. As Christians, our job is to make the
world a better place. We're not supposed to just sit around and wait to go to
heaven with Jesus. We are to make the world a better place by suppressing
the bad that's all around us. Faithfulness is about doing something consistently. Like salt is consistently salty, we are to spread God's goodness around
us consistently. Faithfully.

How can you faithfully spread God's goodness? Here are some ideas for
things that you can do:

- Befriend someone who is lonely. It may be an elderly person who lives alone, another kid on the playground, or an animal without a home. Befriending the lonely makes the world better, and anyone can do it.

- Serve the poor. You can do this by collecting money for a ministry that helps people by giving bags of gift cards and mittens to homeless people or giving toys to orphans.
- Do random acts of kindness. Make your brother's bed, empty the dishwasher, or help clean up.
- Pray for others. Praying for others is one of the best ways to make the world better, and it's also the easiest because you're asking God to do the work.

When you choose to serve others instead of yourself, you are faithfully making the world a better place. You're being salty salt, spreading God's goodness all the time.

DISCUSSION STARTER

- What is one small thing you can do to make the world a better place today?
- What is one thing our family can do regularly to make the world a better place?

PRAYER

Jesus, please show us what it means to be the salt of the earth. Please give us the power to follow you faithfully so we can make this world a better place. Amen.

DAY 77

CONSTANT LIGHT

"You are the light of the world—like a city on a hilltop that
cannot be hidden. No one lights a lamp and then puts it under a
basket. Instead, a lamp is placed on a stand, where it gives light
to everyone in the house. In the same way, let your good
deeds shine out for all to see, so that everyone will
praise your heavenly Father."
(MATTHEW 5:14–16)

Our sun is so important for our world. It brings heat and light and causes plants to grow. Without it, we'd be stumbling around in the darkness, frozen and starving. Thankfully, our sun shines every day, all day and night.

People used to believe the sun traveled around the earth. They thought it traveled the sky from east to west like a fiery chariot racing the same track every day before disappearing under the earth for the night. Of course, now we know it only looks like the sun is scooting across the sky because the earth itself is turning.

The sun is a picture of faithfulness. The sun faithfully shines even when you can't see it. You can't stop it from shining any more than you can stop the planet from turning on its axis. Even if you chose to hide away in the dark, the sun would still be shining up above.

A sun that only shone for part of the day wouldn't be much good, would it? What would happen if the sun took a nap every time it was night in your part of the world? The other side of the world would be terribly chilly and dark.

Jesus is the capital-L Light of the World. He is like the sun, faithfully bringing joy and peace and life to our world. But Jesus also called his followers the light of the world. Our light is more like that of the moon. Just like the moon doesn't have light of its own and simply reflects the light of the sun, so you and I are meant to reflect the light and love of Jesus. The moon might not seem very bright in the daytime, just like you might not feel like the love you share is very much, but the moon can light the way perfectly well on a dark night.

Just like the moon, you and I can faithfully shine Jesus's light in a hurting world. We can listen to people who are sad, share with others, and do the kind of things Jesus did when he was on earth. We can reflect the capital-L Light of the World and let our good deeds shine out for all to see.

DISCUSSION STARTER

- How has someone showed God's light and love to you?
- How would you like to show God's light and love to others?

PRAYER

Thank you, Jesus, for being the Light of the World. Please fill us with your light so we can faithfully reflect your love and truth to everyone we meet. Amen.

DAY 78

A SIGN OF FAITHFULNESS

Then Jesus uttered another loud cry and breathed his last. And
the curtain in the sanctuary of the Temple was torn in two, from
top to bottom.
(MARK 15:37–38)

In the beginning, people had a perfect relationship with God. As you know,
they messed it up, and so have you and I. Our sin keeps us from God because
he is perfect and can't be close to sin.

In Old Testament times, God solved this problem through the sacrificial
system: people sacrificed an animal at the temple and God forgave them.
But it wasn't a perfect system—every time they sinned, they had to sacrifice
again. Plus, only special people could meet with God: high priests.

The place where the high priest met with God was separated from the rest
of the temple by a thick, colorful curtain. For a thousand years, this curtain
hung between the main part of the temple and the Most Holy Place.

The curtain was basically a "Keep Out or Die" sign, reminding everyone
that they weren't good enough to be with God. In order to go behind the
curtain, the high priest made sacrifices to God so his sins, and the sins of all
Israel, would be forgiven. Only then could he go behind the curtain to offer
another sacrifice to God. He had to do this every year because everyone kept
on sinning.

That colorful curtain was still there in Jesus's day, telling everyone to Keep
Out or Die. Here's the problem: The Bible says the death of animals can never
take away sins. Over and again, the high priests offered sacrifices so God
could forgive them, but it never really worked. But God still planned to solve
the problem.

Jesus was the perfect sacrifice because he was human, and he was also
God. God proved that he accepted this perfect sacrifice the moment that Jesus

breathed his last. How? He ripped up the "Keep Out or Die" sign from top to bottom, as easily as you rip a tissue. No human could rip a curtain that thick, especially not from the top! When God ripped that curtain, he showed that he was faithful to fulfill his promises to bring us back to him.

We no longer have to make constant animal sacrifices to be forgiven, and the way to be with God is no longer blocked by a "Keep Out or Die" sign.

Now you and I all have the same job as the priests: to meet with God faithfully. The Bible says, "We can boldly enter heaven's Most Holy Place because of the blood of Jesus. By his death, Jesus opened a new and life-giving way through the curtain into the Most Holy Place" (Hebrews 10:19–20). Isn't that amazing? We don't need to be shy to meet with God, and we don't have to make some big sacrifice either. We just get to meet with our incredible God every day. We can be faithful to God because he is faithful to us.

DISCUSSION STARTER

- Reread Hebrews 10:19–20. What can we do in the Most Holy Place? What does it mean that we can do this?
- Would you like to say something to God in response to his faithfulness?

PRAYER

Thank you, God, for keeping your promise to fix our relationship by sending Jesus. Thank you for proving that you love us and forgive us by ripping up the "Keep Out or Die" sign. Please teach us to be faithful like you are faithful. Amen.

DAY 79

PROMISE KEEPER

The angel spoke to the women. "Don't be afraid!" he said. "I know you are looking for Jesus, who was crucified. He isn't here! He is risen from the dead, just as he said would happen."
(MATTHEW 28:5–6)

Have you ever made a promise to someone? Sometimes promises are fun, like promising to keep a surprise party a secret. Sometimes promises are bad, like promising not to tell that an adult has hurt you. And sometimes promises are incredibly insane, like if I promised I would take you to the moon.

In the Bible, Jesus kept making the same promise over and over. Can you guess what it was?

Here's what he said: "Then Jesus began to tell them that the Son of Man must suffer many terrible things and be rejected by the elders, the leading priests, and the teachers of religious law. He would be killed, but three days later he would rise from the dead" (Mark 8:31).

Over and over, Jesus promised that he would be killed and rise from the dead. But no one understood. His followers acted totally surprised when he was arrested and killed, even though Jesus had promised it so many times. I guess no one wants to believe a depressing promise like that.

Jesus kept his promise because he knew that to be faithful to God's plan, he was going to have to go through with sacrificing his life. Even when no one else around him understood what he was doing, Jesus was faithful.

About a hundred years ago, a pastor named Richard Wurmbrand decided that he also would be faithful to God no matter what. When the government made it illegal to go to church, Pastor Wurmbrand kept inviting people to meet so they could read the Bible and pray. On the way to church one day, he was arrested and sent to jail. While he was there, he was beaten, burned, and locked in a box, but he refused to stop being faithful to Jesus. He created sermons to himself and communicated with other prisoners by tapping on the walls in code called Morse Code. Finally, after fourteen years in jail, some churches paid a ransom so he could be set free.

Not everyone is as faithful as Pastor Wurmbrand. Even Jesus's best friends abandoned him. But the Bible tells us something amazing about Jesus: "If we are unfaithful, he remains faithful, for he cannot deny who he is" (2 Timothy 2:13).

Whether we're as faithful as Pastor Wurmbrand or as unfaithful as the disciples when things get tough, Jesus is still faithful to us because that's who he is. So whether your uncle says you're crazy for believing the Bible or your friends want you to break the rules, remember that Jesus, your faithful friend, is always with you. He can help you be faithful to your beliefs, faithful to obeying your parents, or faithful any other time you're struggling with doing the right thing.

DISCUSSION STARTER

- Has there ever been a time when you were afraid to say you were a Christian? Ask for forgiveness, and allow God's faithfulness to wash over you.

PRAYER

Jesus, please forgive us for the many times we've been unfaithful to you. Thank you for always being faithful to us and for helping us grow in the fruit of faithfulness. Amen.

DAY 80

FAITHFUL PRESENCE

"Be sure of this: I am with you always,
even to the end of the age."
(MATTHEW 28:20)

Have you ever had to say goodbye to someone forever? Maybe a friend moved across the country or an elderly family member passed away. When you say goodbye to someone forever, can you also promise to be with them forever? That doesn't make much sense, does it?

Just as he was about to head to heaven to sit at the right hand of God the Father, Jesus did just that. He stood on a mountain with his disciples and promised that he would always be with them . . . and then he left and was taken into heaven.

Hold the phone. That makes no sense, right? If I promised to be with you forever then disappeared, I would be a liar, wouldn't I? No one can possibly be with someone and leave them at the same time. But the same promise that makes me a liar was completely possible for Jesus to fulfill. See, Jesus, the Son of God, was heading back to heaven. But he also promised to send his Spirit to be with the disciples.

The Spirit has a few names. Sometimes called the Holy Ghost, the Holy Spirit, or the Spirit of Christ, Jesus's Spirit is the part of the Trinity who lives in believers. He helps us pray, share about Jesus, and grow in the fruit of the Spirit.

If you don't sense the Holy Spirit living in you, there may be two reasons:

1. You won't have Jesus's Spirit living in you if you haven't truly accepted that Jesus died for your sins. The Holy Spirit will only live in you if you want him to, and if you haven't chosen to accept God's forgiveness, he won't be there.

2. You might not be looking for the Spirit. It's possible to have God's Spirit working in you and not even notice because you don't know what to look for. Because you've been reading this devotional, now you know that you can watch for the fruit of the Spirit as evidence that the Holy Spirit is with you.

Did you show love to someone who was mean? That's you growing in love. Did you look for something to thank God for even when everything was bad? That's you growing in joy. Did you remind your mom that she could trust God when she was worried? That's you growing in peace. Did you bite your tongue instead of yelling at your brother? That's you growing in patience. Were you kind to someone who didn't deserve it? That's you growing in kindness. Did you choose to obey the teacher when everyone else in the class was disobeying? That's you growing in goodness. Did you hold your baby cousin gently instead of squeezing really hard? That's you growing in gentleness. Did you wait for supper instead of begging for a snack? That's you growing in self-control.

Wow, so much growth! All of those choices are evidence that the Holy Spirit is faithfully working in you, helping you be faithful too.

DISCUSSION STARTER

- Have you noticed evidence that you are growing in one of the fruits of the Spirit?
- Have you noticed evidence that I am growing in one of the fruits of the Spirit?

PRAYER

God, thank you for your faithfulness. Take the truths we have learned and plant them deep in our hearts so they grow the fruit of faithfulness in our lives. Amen.

GENTLENESS

HANDS-ON GROWTH ACTIVITIES

Use these activities as a hands-on supplement to the daily devotions. You can add in one per day, flip to this page for an idea only on days when you have a few extra minutes, or use a few of the activities each Sunday.

Memorize it: Memorize Philippians 4:5 together over the next two weeks.

Write it: Write out Philippians 4:5 in bubble letters and hang it on your wall.

Draw it: Draw a picture of a powerful person or animal being super gentle with someone who is weak.

Pray it: Pray a breath prayer: As you breathe in, say, "You are near," and as you breathe out, say, "your gentleness is here."

Research it: Hosea 11 shows God's reaction to Israel when they've disobeyed him repeatedly. Which verses show power, and which show gentleness?

Imagine it: Close your eyes, and imagine that your friend is having a really bad day. Then your friend accidentally steps on your foot really hard. Imagine Jesus is beside you. How does he help you remain gentle?

Play it: Play the "gentle game" with a family member. One person closes their eyes, and the other has to touch them as gently as possible. What part of the body did they touch? (No cheating here!)

Sing it: Make up a song about God's gentleness.

Ask it: What would be different if our God wasn't a gentle God?

Speak it: Say Philippians 4:5 in a loud, powerful voice. Then imagine you are holding a baby bird and say it again.

For Bible verse printables and other activities,
please visit fruitofthespiritbook.com.

DAY 81

GENTLE MESSIAH

"Look at my Servant, whom I have chosen.
He is my Beloved, who pleases me.
I will put my Spirit upon him,
and he will proclaim justice to the nations.
He will not fight or shout
or raise his voice in public.
He will not crush the weakest reed
or put out a flickering candle.
Finally he will cause justice to be victorious."
(MATTHEW 12:18–20)

Our church always hosts a Christmas Eve service. At the end, they turn out the lights and light a single candle. The pastor takes that candle to the front row, tips it, and lights someone else's candle. Faces glow with joy as the flame gets passed from one row to the next.

One year, my son whispered to me in a panic. All the other candles flickered brightly, but his had mysteriously gone out. (Although it actually wasn't that big a mystery since he was blowing on it.)

I leaned over with my candle and relit his flame. "It's a good thing I'm right here, huh?" I said with a wink. He beamed brighter than the flame.

Today's verses are a quote from a prophecy written hundreds of years before Jesus. The prophecy was given by God to Isaiah. God showed Isaiah what the Messiah was going to be like. Do you remember the part about the candle? Reread that line: "He will not crush the weakest reed or put out a flickering candle" (Matthew 12:20).

Sometimes our faith is like a flickering flame. You might have experienced some really hard things in your life. You might be dealing with anxiety or bullying, or maybe you're having trouble learning something important.

These things can make it hard to have faith in Jesus. Even if your life is pretty easy, it's important to remember that lots of kids do have a hard life.

But guess what? In his gentleness, Jesus doesn't yell at you. He treats you like I treated my son. I relit his candle from mine because I love him.

Jesus won't get mad at you for making a mistake (or even lots of mistakes). He is full of gentleness and care for people who are hurting. Imagine him coming close, giving you a hug, and saying, "It's a good thing I'm right here, huh?" And as you learn to trust his gentleness, you'll find yourself being gentler with those around you who make mistakes.

DISCUSSION STARTER

- What character traits are shown in this passage?
- We often think of gentleness as being weakness, but gentleness is actually best shown when someone very powerful keeps their power under control. How does Jesus show power-under-control gentleness in this passage?

PRAYER

Jesus, thank you for being gentle. Thank you that you don't crush those who are hurting or blow out the flame of our faith when we're having trouble believing in you. Please show us your gentleness this week. Amen.

DAY 82

PEACEFUL KING

"Tell the people of Jerusalem,
'Look, your King is coming to you.
He is humble, riding on a donkey—
riding on a donkey's colt.'"
(MATTHEW 21:5)

If you were announcing yourself as king or queen for the first time, what would you do?

Here's what I would do. First, I would get a big warhorse and make it look really fancy. I might even braid its mane or dip its tail in gold. (Is that a thing? It should be a thing.) Next, I would command my big army to march behind me to prove that I'm a great leader. Then I would hire a band to play exciting music in front of me and a choir to sing songs about how amazing I am. Last, I'd definitely tell everyone I was coming and promise lots of candy to everyone who hooted and hollered as my big parade came into the city.

Doesn't that sound like a great way to enter a city? You would think Jesus, as God's Son, might have done something like that. I mean, he has angel armies, so surely a single horse with a golden tail wouldn't be too much for him.

But no, that's not what Jesus did. Instead, he sat on a borrowed cloak on a borrowed donkey and rode into Jerusalem surrounded by just his friends.

No one knew he was coming, but something about this oddball entrance caused a big ruckus. The people of Jerusalem laid their coats on the ground in front of the donkey and waved palm branches, shouting praises to God.

This is what gentleness is all about. Some people think gentleness is weakness, but it's actually the very opposite. Gentleness is great power . . . under control. Someone who is gentle doesn't need to prove they are strong. They already know they're strong, and they choose to keep their strength under control so they don't hurt others.

Jesus didn't need to prove he was strong. He had already healed tons of people, brought others back to life, walked on water, stopped a storm, and fed thousands of people with five loaves of bread and two fish. He knew he was strong. He didn't need to prove it. Instead, he chose to keep his strength under control and enter Jerusalem on a donkey in order to show what God is like.

You might not feel like a strong person, but the most powerful being in the universe loves you and is with you all the time. When you feel like you have to prove your strength by joining a group of kids who are making fun of someone, or by pushing a little kid at the park, remember that God is with you. You don't need to prove anything. Instead, the Holy Spirit can help you keep your strength under control and show gentleness instead.

DISCUSSION STARTER

- Read Matthew 21:1–5. In what way(s) did Jesus show his power in these verses? In what ways did he show that his great power was under control?
- Tell about an area of your life where you have a hard time being gentle.

PRAYER

I know you are powerful, Jesus. Thank you for keeping your power under control and being gentle with us. Help us to learn to keep our strength under control too. Amen.

DAY 83

GENTLENESS WINS THE DAY

When Jesus came by, he looked up at Zacchaeus and called him
by name. "Zacchaeus!" he said. "Quick, come down! I must be a
guest in your home today."
(LUKE 19:5)

Have you ever been called a name? My third grade teacher called me a
shrimp, and I never got over it.

I bet Zacchaeus was called a lot of names in his life. Maybe Shrimp was
one of them, since one of the only things we know about him is that he was
short. Can you imagine a Bible story about you, where one of the main things
the author wrote down was that you were short or had frizzy hair or a big
nose? How embarrassing.

But we can also guess Zacchaeus was called some other things. He probably heard "cheater" and "thief" muttered behind his back. Zacchaeus was a
tax collector. No one liked tax collectors because they worked for the enemy:
Rome. Rome already demanded a lot of money from the people of Israel, and
tax collectors were known for taking a little (or a lot) extra. They were cheaters and thieves, and everyone knew it. Zacchaeus wasn't accidentally taking
extra money from the people of Jericho; he knew exactly what he was doing.

You might expect that God's Son, the one who knows what is in our hearts,
would be a little annoyed with Zacchaeus, the shrimpy cheater. He deserved
to go to jail or at least get a good lecture from the Son of God, who hates cheating. But even though God hates cheating, he loves cheaters. No, he doesn't
love what they do. But he does love them and knows they can be saved.

So, when Zacchaeus climbed a tree just to get a peek at Jesus, Jesus
didn't waggle his finger and give this shrimpy cheater a much-needed lecture. Instead, Jesus invited himself over for a visit. This is such an amazing
example of Jesus's gentleness. He had every right to punish Zacchaeus for

stealing from the Jews, but he chose to control his power and show gentleness instead.

If Jesus had given Zacchaeus a lecture or a punishment, Zacchaeus probably would have gotten angry. But because Jesus showed gentleness, Zacchaeus's heart changed. That very night, Zacchaeus stood up and promised to give a lot of money back to those he had cheated and to give half his possessions to the poor.

Imagine this: You're at your desk working out some word problems in math, and you notice the girl next to you looking at your work. You could tell the teacher. The cheater deserves to get in trouble, right? Or, if you're allowed to talk, you could turn to the girl and help her understand the question. That would be a way to control your power and show gentleness instead, and maybe even make a new friend.

DISCUSSION STARTER

- Have you ever thought you were going to get in big trouble, then experienced gentleness instead?

PRAYER

Thank you, Jesus, for being gentle with us even when we sin. Help us to be gentle like you are gentle. Amen.

DAY 84

NO CONDEMNATION

Jesus stood up again and said
to the woman, "Where are your accusers?
Didn't even one of them condemn you?"
"No, Lord," she said. And Jesus said,
"Neither do I. Go and sin no more."
(JOHN 8:10–11)

Have you ever heard the saying, "Sticks and stones may break my bones, but words will never hurt me"? It's true that sticks and stones really can break bones. In fact, in Bible times, when someone behaved especially bad, they were sometimes punished by having stones thrown at them . . . until they died. Yikes.

One day, Jesus was teaching at the temple. A whole crowd was around him, listening. Suddenly, people started murmuring and moving as a group of religious leaders pushed their way through. They dragged a woman behind them. Can you imagine a group of angry teachers yanking a woman along by her hair? Pretty messed up. I imagine them shoving her down in front of Jesus, and the lady weeping on the ground with her hands covering her head.

These leaders knew they were right. This woman had committed a great sin, and she deserved to be punished. They wanted to stone her, and they wanted Jesus to admit that she deserved to be stoned to death. If they couldn't get their way, they hoped Jesus would at least say something that would make the people think he was a big faker.

Instead of getting angry at her or the Pharisees, Jesus just bent down and started writing in the dust. No one knows what he wrote, but some people think he started writing a list of sins those teachers themselves were guilty of. When he stood up, he simply said, "Let the one who has never sinned throw the first stone!" (John 8:7). Every single one of them walked away.

When it was just Jesus and the woman, he finally spoke to her. I imagine her slowly peeking out from behind her hands, face dirty with dust and tears, surprised that no one was left to chuck a rock at her. Maybe she expected Jesus to yell. Instead, he said he didn't condemn her. "Go and sin no more," he said.

Jesus didn't have to be gentle with this woman. She had sinned, and we know that sin separates us from God. But instead of yelling at her or punishing her, Jesus was gentle. The Bible doesn't tell us what happened after, but I think she probably reacted to Jesus's gentleness just like Zacchaeus did . . . with a changed life.

It's so easy to look at kids who make bad choices and condemn them. That boy who threw a chair across the room? *He must be crazy.* That girl who gossips behind everyone's back? *She's so mean.* But being gentle includes not condemning others, just like Jesus. You don't have to be best friends with kids who are making bad choices, but God can help you be gentle with them.

DISCUSSION STARTER

- Tell about a time when you wanted someone else to get punished. What happened to them?
- When the Holy Spirit lives in us, he changes us to be more like Jesus, but we have to choose to join in! How can you choose gentleness this week?

PRAYER

Jesus, thank you for your gentleness toward sinners. Please help us choose gentleness toward others, just like you do. Amen.

DAY 85

KISSING BABIES

Jesus called for the children and said to the disciples, "Let the children come to me. Don't stop them! For the Kingdom of God belongs to those who are like these children. I tell you the truth, anyone who doesn't receive the Kingdom of God like a child will never enter it."
(LUKE 18:16–17)

Remember your first birthday? A funny tradition that is popular now is called a cake smash, where one-year-olds are plunked down in front of a big cake, and they get to cover themselves with crumbs and icing. Sounds yummy, right?

In ancient Jewish times, no one did cake smashes for a baby's first birthday (as far as we know, anyway). But some Jewish moms liked to bring their babies to an important rabbi (teacher) on the little one's first birthday so the rabbi could bless the child. That's likely what's happening in these verses. Jesus was an important rabbi, and the moms were there with their babies, hoping for a blessing, like some moms today hold up their babies for a celebrity to kiss.

The disciples didn't like this. Jesus was always surrounded by people, and he didn't need snotty toddlers shoved in his face. So the disciples shooed the parents away. They *knew* Jesus had far more important things to do than bless babies. Take them to the rabbi down the road!

But instead of pushing away the parents or yelling at the disciples, Jesus chose the way of gentle strength. He explained to his disciples that the Kingdom of Heaven belongs to children and that their faith is an example for us to follow. But he didn't whack them over the head with it.

Jesus could have called down some angels to force everyone to stop talking, then yelled, "Now listen up! I'm the one who decides who gets close to me and who gets into the Kingdom of Heaven, so y'all just be quiet and listen!" But Jesus didn't use his power to call down heavenly help. He didn't yell at anyone, either. He kept his power under control and showed gentleness by inviting the kids closer. He also used that moment to lovingly teach his disciples instead of giving a harsh rebuke.

Jesus had infinite power, but when he was interrupted, he chose to kiss babies and gently teach his disciples. I don't know about you, but I am not always this gentle when I'm interrupted from important work. I get a little angry and want to say mean words. How about you? When you're almost at the next level in your video game, focusing on an art project, or creating the most amazing block tower on the planet, it's hard to be gentle when you're interrupted. You probably want to yell or stomp or slam a door. But with God's help, both you and I can choose the gentle way.

DISCUSSION STARTER

- Who is the gentlest person you know?
- How do you treat others when you're interrupted?
- How can Jesus help you be gentler?

PRAYER

Thank you, Jesus, for your amazing gentleness. Help us receive the kingdom of God like a little child. And help us invite others in through gentleness. Amen.

DAY 86

UPSIDE-DOWN KINGDOM

His disciples began arguing about which of them was the
greatest. But Jesus knew their thoughts, so he brought a little
child to his side. Then he said to them, "Anyone who welcomes a
little child like this on my behalf welcomes me, and anyone
who welcomes me also welcomes my Father who sent me.
Whoever is the least among you is the greatest."
(LUKE 9:46–48)

What would you do if you were the Most Important Person in a kingdom?
Would you ask someone else to do the jobs you dislike, like clean up the bathroom, do your schoolwork, or even bring you a nice, cold lemonade? It sure
seems like being the Most Important Person would be amazing.

In these verses, the disciples were fighting over who would be the Most
Important Person in Jesus's kingdom. The problem, and the thing they really
didn't understand, is that Jesus's kingdom isn't like earthly kingdoms. Some
people call the kingdom of God an "upside-down kingdom" because in it,
everything is upside down!

In earthly kingdoms, people who are the biggest and strongest and smartest are the leaders, and everyone else serves them. In God's kingdom, the
way to become a leader is to welcome those who are smaller than you and
to serve others. In God's kingdom, the people who are normally last get to
go first.

Think about a time you've lined up for something. Are you one of the kids
who shoulders your way toward the front of the line in order to get the first
scoop of ice cream? In God's kingdom, the kid waiting patiently at the back
gets to go first. Actually, that's not quite true. The kid sitting in the corner
who was too shy to even line up gets to go first!

Doesn't that seem wild? In these verses, Jesus was once again teaching his

GENTLENESS

---

disciples about gentleness...

disciples about gentleness. Gentleness is when we have power but choose to control it so we don't hurt others.

For example, let's go back to our ice-cream lineup. Let's imagine you're the biggest kid in the lineup. It would be easy to push your way to the front of the line. But a gentle kid would choose not to do that. The gentle kid would let other kids go first and might even go get the shy kid in the corner and stand with him in line.

That's what Jesus was talking about when he said, "Whoever is the least among you is the greatest" (Luke 9:48).

DISCUSSION STARTER

- Tell about a time when you were gentle.
- What did Jesus teach the disciples about being the greatest? What does that have to do with gentleness?

PRAYER

Thank you, God, for being the biggest and strongest and smartest but still choosing to be gentle. Help us understand what it looks like to be a part of your upside-down kingdom. Amen.

DAY 87

GENTLE YOKE

Jesus said, "Come to me, all of you who are weary and carry
heavy burdens, and I will give you rest. Take my yoke upon you.
Let me teach you, because I am humble and gentle at heart, and
you will find rest for your souls. For my yoke is easy to bear, and
the burden I give you is light."
(MATTHEW 11:28–30)

If you had to carry a couch from one house to another house, how would
you do it? Maybe you would get your back under it and hoist it up, or you'd
tip it on its side to wrestle it out the door. Maybe you'd have to find a chain
saw and chop it into pieces! But here's what I would do: I'd call a professional
mover to do it for me.

No matter how strong you are, there's always going to be something that
is too heavy for you to lift. This reminds me of what Jesus said in today's
passage.

Jesus used a word picture to help us understand what he does for us.

A *yoke* is a wooden frame that farmers put on the necks of animals to link
them together. Usually, a young animal was put beside an older animal, who
would train the younger one.

In this word picture, Jesus isn't the farmer placing a yoke on you. Our God
doesn't load us down with expectations. Instead, Jesus is like the older animal that carries most of the weight while showing you how to live.

In fact, that's exactly the point of this whole book. We have discovered that
Jesus doesn't threaten you, saying, "Be gentler, or else!" or "I'm sick of your
impatience! It's time for a spanking."

Instead, Jesus picks up your yoke of sin. (That yoke, by the way, was created by humans, not by Jesus.) He puts your yoke on his own back and invites
you to walk with him. Jesus does the heavy lifting while showing you how

to live more like him. His yoke is easy and his burden is light because he's doing most of the work.

What work is left for you to do? Jesus said, "This is the only work God wants from you: Believe in the one he has sent" (John 6:29). Here's another way to think about it: your work is to give Jesus your yoke and let him help you carry it.

Since I know you aren't literally carrying a yoke on your shoulders, what might this look like in your real life? Let's imagine you got into trouble at home because you used your mom's phone without permission. You might feel really bad about it for a long time. Whenever you look at the phone, you get a sick feeling in your stomach because you know you did something wrong. Jesus doesn't want you to hold on to that bad feeling. Letting Jesus carry your yoke would mean saying, "I'm sorry" to God (and your mom), then letting Jesus take away the guilty feeling. Your job is just to believe that you are forgiven, and let the Holy Spirit change you so you don't make that same mistake again.

DISCUSSION STARTER

- What is something that feels like a heavy burden to you?
- Let's take a few minutes to give that burden to Jesus.

PRAYER

Jesus, you are so gentle but so strong. Thank you for carrying the burden for us, and for helping us live our lives well. Amen.

DAY 88

GENTLE SPIRIT

He returned to the disciples and found them asleep. He said to
Peter, "Couldn't you watch with me even one hour?
Keep watch and pray, so that you will not give
in to temptation. For the spirit is willing,
but the body is weak!"
(MATTHEW 26:40–41)

Have you ever promised yourself that next time someone annoys you, you
will be gentle and kind? You promise yourself that you'll count to ten, take a
deep breath, and keep your mean words inside. But instead you end up yelling at the annoying person or throwing a ball of socks at their head. Maybe
you even rattle the house when you slam the door in their face!

That is exactly what Jesus meant when he said, "The spirit is willing, but
the body is weak." That phrase means that even when part of you really
wants to do the right thing, your sinful mind wants to take the easy way
out. For instance, when your dad tells you it's time to stop watching vid-
eos online, part of you might *want* to obey, but your sinful mind wants to
just keep watching. "Ignore him," your sinful mind says. "It's just one little
video." Or it says, "He doesn't understand you. You should scream at him!"
That, my friend, is sin. And sin is exactly why Jesus came to earth.

Before he was arrested, Jesus was in an olive grove praying, trying to
deal with his own "spirit is willing but the body is weak" situation. Jesus
was scared to be crucified, to be separated from his Father. He hoped his
Father had another way. Three times he asked his best friends to stay awake
and pray for him, and three times they fell asleep. Some friends, huh? They
couldn't even comfort their best friend on his worst day.

My sinful mind would say, "Try stuffing olives in their noses. Maybe that
will keep them awake." Obviously, that wouldn't be very Christlike. Jesus

was exhausted and afraid, but in the midst of this, he was still gentle with his sleepy disciples.

Jesus knows that our spirits are willing but our bodies are weak. That's exactly why he died. Through his death we are forgiven, and through his resurrection we are given power to choose a better way. We don't have to keep listening to our sinful minds. We can choose to listen to the words of Jesus instead.

And here's what he's whispering to you: "I love you. I forgive you. Come walk with me and talk with me and live your life with me."

DISCUSSION STARTER

- Tell about something bad you've tried to stop doing. Have you been able to stop? If not, remember that Jesus died for your forgiveness and sent the Holy Spirit to help you choose a better way.
- What are some things you can do to help remember to listen to Jesus's words instead of your sinful mind?

PRAYER

Thank you, Jesus, for your constant gentleness with us. Please continue to grow gentleness inside us as we get to know you better. Amen.

DAY 89

GENTLE STRENGTH

Jesus fully realized all that was going to happen to him,
so he stepped forward to meet them. "Who are you looking for?"
he asked. "Jesus the Nazarene," they replied. "I AM he," Jesus
said. (Judas, who betrayed him, was standing with them.) As
Jesus said "I AM he," they all drew back and fell to the ground!
(JOHN 18:4–6)

Imagine you are in the garden with Jesus. It is dark, and he has been praying. Suddenly you see lights bobbing up the hill toward you. Your heart skips a beat, because you know it's dangerous to be with Jesus in Jerusalem right now. Your friend Judas busts through the trees, leading a group of soldiers and religious leaders. They carry torches, lanterns, . . . and weapons. This is not a friendly visit.

You have a sword, but your group is outnumbered. Jesus asks, "What do you want?" He's so calm, which is the total opposite of how you feel right now. Your head is buzzing, wondering if you'll need to fight your way out.

"Jesus of Nazareth," they reply. It feels like you have rocks in your stomach. It's really happening.

Then something crazy happens. Jesus replies, "I AM he," and everyone steps backward then falls down!

What happened there? God's name is "I AM," and Jesus claimed this name as his own. He claimed to be God and had the power to prove it.

Jesus clearly had infinite power at his disposal, and in that moment, he showed who was really in charge of the situation. All Jesus had to do was speak a word and it landed everyone on their backs! And yet they picked themselves up and arrested him anyway. He allowed them to arrest him, put him on trial, and kill him, because Jesus is gentle.

When someone has no power, they don't need to be gentle. A tiny baby can't hurt a grown human, but a grown human can kill a tiny baby if they're not gentle. It's the strong, not the weak, who must be gentle.

You may not feel strong today. But no matter how many people are stronger or more powerful than you, nearly everyone has someone who is weaker and needs gentleness. Maybe you have a younger sibling who can't read very well, and you need to be gentle when you help him so you don't hurt his feelings. When you're at the park, you can be gentle with the littler kids around you, making sure you don't knock them over when you're playing tag. Ask Jesus for eyes to see who is weaker than you and for the power to be gentle toward them.

DISCUSSION STARTER

- Name someone who is stronger than you. How would you like that person to treat you?
- Name someone who is weaker than you. How can you be gentle toward that person?

PRAYER

Thank you, Jesus, for holding back your great power most of the time! Please fill us with your Spirit so we can become gentler toward those who are weaker than us. Amen.

DAY 90

LION AND LAMB

"Do not resist an evil person! If someone slaps you on the right
cheek, offer the other cheek also. If you are sued in court and
your shirt is taken from you, give your coat, too. If a soldier
demands that you carry his gear for a mile, carry it two miles."
(MATTHEW 5:39–41)

When you read these verses, did something inside you think, "I could never
do that"? It feels like weakness to us, doesn't it? No one likes to feel weak.

Would you believe me if I told you that what Jesus taught in this passage
is actually a show of power?

In Jesus's example of getting slapped on the cheek, a weak person would
crumple into a ball and cry in the corner. A powerful person would slap back,
maybe with an extra punch thrown in. But it actually takes enormous power
and self-confidence to stand tall, refuse to take revenge, and turn the other
cheek.

In the Bible, Jesus is called the Lion of Judah. He's powerful like a lion
and has the ability to immediately force every human being to bow down
and worship him. But he doesn't. Jesus is also called the Lamb, because he
willingly allowed his enemy to slap him on the other cheek . . . and nail him
to a cross.

Jesus didn't go to the cross because he was weak. He allowed himself to be
killed because he had a mission to accomplish.

The apostle John received a vision of heaven. He wrote:

I heard the voices of thousands and millions of angels around the
throne and of the living beings and the elders. And they sang in a
mighty chorus:

"Worthy is the Lamb who was slaughtered—
to receive power and riches
and wisdom and strength
and honor and glory and blessing." (Revelation 5:11–12)

No one worships a weakling! Jesus is not sometimes the Lion and some-times the Lamb. He is 100 percent Lion of Judah. He has always had the power to blast his enemies to smithereens or turn our planet to dust and start again. But because he is also 100 percent Lamb of God, he chose to turn the other cheek and allow his own death, because he knew his death and resurrection were the only way to a relationship with you.

Every day, you have the choice to react out of weakness, power, or gen-tleness. Choosing gentleness isn't going to be easy. If someone slaps me on the cheek, my first instinct won't be to turn the other cheek. And honestly? I get it wrong a lot of times, and so will you. We'll mess up. We'll act out of weakness or pretend to be powerful instead of showing gentleness. But Jesus walked the path of gentleness so you could be forgiven. Even though that path is impossible for us to travel on our own, never forget that because of the sacrifice of the Lamb of God, the incredible power of the Lion of Judah lives inside you.

DISCUSSION STARTER

- Has anyone ever slapped you, or taken something from you, or forced you to do something? How did you respond? Ask Jesus for the power to choose gentleness next time something like this happens.
- Are there times when you shouldn't respond in gentleness?

PRAYER

Jesus, you are Lion and Lamb, powerful and gentle. Please teach us to use our power gently. Amen.

SELF-CONTROL

HANDS-ON GROWTH ACTIVITIES

Use these activities as a hands-on supplement to the daily devotions. You can add in one per day, flip to this page for an idea only on days when you have a few extra minutes, or use a few of the activities each Sunday.

Memorize it: Memorize 2 Timothy 1:7 together over the next two weeks.

Write it: Write 2 Timothy 1:7 in fancy letters. Hang it on your wall.

Draw it: Draw the tastiest dessert you can imagine. Would it be hard to have self-control with that dessert?

Pray it: Pray a breath prayer: As you breathe in, say, "You have not given me a spirit of fear . . ." and as you breathe out, say, "but of power, of love, and of self-control."

Research it: How does God show self-control in Exodus 33?

Imagine it: Close your eyes and imagine that you are getting super-duper angry. Now imagine Jesus standing right next to you. What does he do or say to help you have self-control?

Play it: Play the smile game! The point of the game is to try to get someone in your family to smile. Choose one person to be the guinea pig, and the rest must do everything possible to make that person smile. Time how long it takes each person to crack a smile.

Sing it: Find (or make up) a song about self-control.

Ask it: What would be different if our God wasn't a self-controlled God?

Speak it: Hide under a table and whisper 2 Timothy 1:7, then stand on a chair and shout it.

For Bible verse printables and other activities,
please visit fruitofthespiritbook.com.

DAY 91

CONTROLLING THE WALLS

Since he himself has gone through suffering and testing, he is
able to help us when we are being tested.
(Hebrews 2:18)

Imagine that your family just bought a new house. Everyone is super excited about it because there's a big park next door, a pond down the street, and a secret trapdoor into the attic for a fort. You pack everything up and drive over to the house, only to realize you have a problem. A big one. There are no walls! There are pillars holding up the roof and even ceilings and floors, but no walls. Why would that be a problem?

Well, if your house had no walls, all the neighborhood raccoons might snuggle with you at bedtime. You might find a lot of mice snacking on crackers in your cupboard. It would get awfully cold at night. And anyone could walk in at any time and steal your special collection, or generally make your life miserable.

The Bible says, "A person without self-control is like a city with broken-down walls" (Proverbs 25:28). Without walls, a house wouldn't be safe. Your enemies could walk right in and take your stuff. Our enemy is sin. This verse says that if we don't have self-control, sin can walk right into our lives and make our lives miserable.

Why is that? Let's imagine you don't have any self-control with caramel candies. If you see a caramel candy in front of you, you eat it, even if someone says you shouldn't. Now, what if you see a tray of caramel candies at the store? You will be tempted to steal one because you already have no self-control with those candies. Unless you're the kind of kid who can walk right by, those caramel candies will be a huge temptation to sin! That kind of sin grows and grows unless God comes in and helps us be more self-controlled.

Jesus knew exactly how it felt to be tempted because he was tempted every day. Just like you and me, he had to say *no* to greed, selfishness, hurting others, and fighting.

What kind of help does Jesus give? First, he promises that "he will not allow the temptation to be more than you can stand. When you are tempted, he will show you a way out so that you can endure" (1 Corinthians 10:13). There will always be a way out, so when you pray, he will help you!

Second, he forgives us when we mess up. I know you're going to mess up, and you can be sure that I'll mess up. But Jesus is always faithful to forgive and help us.

DISCUSSION STARTER

- What kind of temptations do you think Jesus had to say no to?
- If your life is like a house, how are your self-control walls doing?

PRAYER

Jesus, I'm so glad you know what we're going through. Thank you for being the perfect example of self-control and also for sending the Spirit to help us build our self-control muscles. Amen.

DAY 92

SWING THAT SWORD

Jesus was led by the Spirit into the wilderness to be tempted
there by the devil. For forty days and forty nights he fasted
and became very hungry. During that time the devil came
and said to him, "If you are the Son of God, tell these
stones to become loaves of bread." But Jesus told him,
"No! The Scriptures say, 'People do not live by bread alone,
but by every word that comes from the mouth of God.'"
(MATTHEW 4:1–4)

How many types of weapons can you think of? Swords, guns, knives, throwing stars, scimitars . . . that's as much as I know about weapons. In your list, did you name the Bible?

Ephesians 6:17 talks about how we can protect ourselves against evil using the armor of God. It says we should "take the sword of the Spirit, which is the word of God." It's kind of weird to think of the Bible as a weapon, isn't it? I mean, it's hard to protect yourself from an enemy with a book. Maybe if it was heavy enough you could knock someone out with it, but normally a book isn't a great weapon to bring to a battle. However, the Word of God isn't just any old book!

The devil came to tempt Jesus when he was weakest. We are often tempted when we are weak too. Maybe you don't understand the math problems you're supposed to hand in, so you look up the answers. Or maybe a kid at the park is being mean to you, so you push him off the equipment. Or you're super-duper hungry, so you sneak the snack your mom told you not to have before supper.

You can use the Word of God like a sword against temptation. You can say a verse like this one: "I can do everything through Christ, who gives me strength" (Philippians 4:13). Or this one: "God blesses those who hunger and thirst for justice, for they will be satisfied" (Matthew 5:6).

This won't always be easy. Unlike us, Jesus was able to use his sword of the Spirit to fight back against the sneaky temptations every single time. Because of that, he was the perfect sacrifice to take the consequences of sin from us. And when he came back to life and went to heaven, he left the Holy Spirit for you and me. Imagine the Holy Spirit like a mechanical arm that helps you swing your own sword of the Spirit against temptations. Nothing can stand against you when you pair the sword of the Spirit with the Holy Spirit.

When you feel stuck, like you have no other choice but to sin, say, "Help me, Jesus!" That's the kind of prayer Jesus loves to answer with a great big YES.

DISCUSSION STARTER

- Tell a Bible verse you have memorized. (If you don't have any memorized, choose a simple one to memorize as a family this week!)

PRAYER

Thank you, Jesus, for showing us what it's like to have self-control but also for giving us the Holy Spirit, so we can actually swing our own sword of the Spirit. Amen.

DAY 93

SWEET TEMPTATION

Next the devil took him to the peak of a very high mountain and
showed him all the kingdoms of the world and their glory.
"I will give it all to you," he said, "if you will
kneel down and worship me."
"Get out of here, Satan," Jesus told him. "For the Scriptures say,
'You must worship the LORD your God and serve only him.'"
(MATTHEW 4:8–10)

In a famous book called *The Lion, the Witch and the Wardrobe*, a boy named
Edmund stumbles into a magical world called Narnia. The first person he
meets in that icy winter world is a beautiful woman with a golden crown,
riding a sledge pulled by reindeer. She says she is the Queen of Narnia and
invites Edmund onto her sledge. She wraps his shivering body in warm furs
and offers him his favorite treat. Edmund is entranced. The queen says he
would make a wonderful prince as heir to her throne. However, this will only
happen if he brings his brother and two sisters to the magical world as well.

If you haven't read the book, this encounter might sound amazing.
Wouldn't you like to be a prince or princess and have your siblings serve
you? But if you have read this book, you'll know that this queen is actually
the evil White Witch who has kept the entire magical country in winter for a
hundred years. She knows the prophecy that says two brothers and two sisters will break her spell and her power over the world, so she wants Edmund
to bring his siblings to her so she can kill all four of them. Edmund doesn't
realize she is evil until much later in the book, after he has made some terrible mistakes.

Just like Edmund, Jesus was tempted. The devil brought Jesus to the top of
a mountain and offered all the kingdoms of the world to Jesus, if only Jesus
would worship him. Just like the White Witch pretending to be queen, the

devil wants to be king of this world, and will do anything to become king. He even tried to get the rightful King to bow down to him!

In Edmund's story, he is also one of the rightful kings. His enemy tries to trick him into following her, and he lets her do it. Why? He wants to believe her because he is selfish.

Thankfully, Jesus didn't behave like Edmund. There is no selfishness in Jesus. He didn't fall for the lies, and he used his weapon, the sword of the Spirit, to battle against the lies. Using the sword of the Spirit (also known as the Bible) is the best way to control yourself in any situation. When you are tempted to behave selfishly, call out to Jesus! He has promised to help you fight temptation.

DISCUSSION STARTER

• Are you more like Edmund or more like Jesus? Why?

PRAYER

Thank you, Jesus, for showing us how to have self-control. Please help us listen to you instead of to the selfishness in our hearts. Amen.

DAY 94

MIND CONTROL

"All these evil things begin inside a person, in the mind: evil
thoughts, sexual immorality, stealing, murder, adultery,
selfishness, doing bad things to other people, lying, doing sinful
things, jealousy, saying bad things about people, pride,
and foolish living."
(MARK 7:21–22 ICB)

Imagine that you have two thermoses in front of you. One thermos is dented
and dirty, like someone threw it down a mountain. The other thermos looks like
it came right off the store shelf. Which thermos would you like to drink from?

Now imagine that I open them up and pour water from the new-looking
thermos into your glass. Ugh! It smells like a teenager's armpit and looks like
seventeen people washed their socks in it. Would you rather try the water
from the dented thermos? I thought so. Let me pour you some. The water in
this thermos is cool and refreshing because it came straight from a waterfall
on a mountain.

Jesus said it's possible for people, just like the thermoses, to look good on the
outside and be full of junk on the inside, at least for a while. You might know
some kids like that. They act perfect in front of teachers and parents, but when
there aren't any adults around, they are nastier than the pointy side of a porcu-
pine. Just like the fancy thermos, the junk on the inside will come out somehow.

Self-control always starts with what's going on in our minds. It's tough to
have a mind that's out of control and have a body that's always in control.

What does it look like to have an out-of-control, junk-filled mind?

Well, you might think a lot about what other people are doing wrong.
Maybe you think, "That's a dumb way to make a paper airplane," or "That's
not how to do that math problem. Dopey kid!" If you're always having pride-
ful thoughts like that, they might ooze out in your words or actions.

Another way to have a junk-filled mind is to only think about yourself. This is called selfishness, and it will always ooze out as putting yourself first. It might look like taking the biggest cookie, taking your brother's favorite sled simply because you want to use it, or refusing to help someone who needs you.

In order to have self-control, we have to let God change the way we think. Romans 12:2 says, "Don't copy the behavior and customs of this world, but let God transform you into a new person by changing the way you think." Only when God cleans us up on the inside can we truly say NO to acting pridefully and selfishly, and YES to self-control.

DISCUSSION STARTER

- What type of mind-junk do you struggle with? (Mark 7:21–23 can help if you're stuck for ideas.)

PRAYER

God, we are sorry for the junk we've let into our minds, like [*use examples from your answers to the discussion starter*]. Please forgive us and transform us by changing the way we think! Amen.

DAY 95

SLOW ANGER

Understand this, my dear brothers and sisters: You must all be
quick to listen, slow to speak, and slow to get angry. Human
anger does not produce the righteousness God desires.
(JAMES 1:19–20)

Has anyone ever said something mean about you or your family? Maybe they
made fun of your name, and it hurt your feelings; or they said something
really nasty about your parents, and it made you as angry as a mama bear
defending her cubs. When others say hurtful things about me, I don't want
to be kind, gentle, or good. It makes me angry, and I want to get revenge, or
argue, or say hurtful words right back.

One time, Jesus met a demon-possessed man who was blind and mute.
Jesus freed him from the demons and healed him so he could see and talk.
When the Pharisees heard about the healing, they said something totally
mean about him. They said, "No wonder he can cast out demons. He gets his
power from Satan, the prince of demons" (Matthew 12:24). They said he was
doing satanic magic! Um, wrong! Jesus wasn't on Satan's team. He was God's
Son, and this was a real miracle from the loving God.

The Pharisees tried to get people to doubt Jesus and doubt God's love and
truth, but Jesus didn't show any anger, and he didn't lose self-control. Jesus
knew what the Pharisees were whispering among themselves. He could have
snapped his fingers and made corn grow out of their ears or even forced them
to bow down to him, but that's not who Jesus is. He didn't react to the hurtful
words. Instead, he showed self-control and explained how he couldn't possibly be working through Satan's power.

Through his life, Jesus constantly showed us what it looks like to be slow
to get angry. Of course, you and I can't be perfect like Jesus was perfect, but
God can help us choose the better way.

Getting angry all the time is like a weed that keeps the other fruits of the Spirit from growing. If we have no self-control, it's tough to be loving, kind, gentle, faithful, patient, or good. But when the Holy Spirit grows self-control in our lives, we'll naturally grow all those other fruits of the Spirit too! As we learn to be slow to anger, it's like we're pulling that weed out so fruits like patience and kindness have a better chance to grow in our lives.

DISCUSSION STARTER

- Share about an area of your life where you're quick to become angry. (If you can't think of a time when this happens to you, ask God to reveal something to you. He will probably give you a thought or a memory of a time you lost your temper.) Let's tell God about it and ask him for self-control the next time that situation comes up.

PRAYER

Jesus, thank you for always being slow to become angry. If you were quick to get angry, we'd all be in trouble! We invite you into our lives. Please help us become quick to listen, slow to speak, and slow to become angry. Amen.

DAY 96

UNSELFISH ANGER

When they arrived back in Jerusalem, Jesus entered the Temple
and began to drive out the people buying and selling animals for
sacrifices. He knocked over the tables of the money changers and
the chairs of those selling doves, and he stopped everyone from
using the Temple as a marketplace.
(MARK 11:15–16)

If I asked you to think of an example of Jesus being self-controlled, I bet it
wouldn't be this part of the Bible! Would you immediately think of Jesus
knocking over tables and chairs? Probably not, because if you or I were
knocking over tables and chairs, it would mean we were either crazy or crazy
angry.

But did you know that Jesus did this twice? The first time, Jesus saw merchants and money changers in the temple, so he took some rope and twisted
it into a whip. I imagine his disciples raising eyebrows at each other behind
his back, wondering what was about to happen. I'm sure none of them predicted he would use the whip to chase merchants from the temple!

Can you imagine this scene? Cattle mooing in fright, sheep bleating, doves
cooing, men shouting, tables skidding and thudding like giants break dancing, and coins clattering all over the stone floor. I also imagine some of those
animals kicked free of their ropes, knocking people over and smashing into
dove cages, causing a blizzard of feathers. Total chaos!

We know that Jesus never sinned, so what he did here wasn't a sin. Our
human anger usually comes from selfishness. Maybe you get angry when
someone takes the last cookie, leaving only just a few crumbs. Or you get
angry when your brother wins the game you wanted to win, or when your
friend doesn't give you the birthday gift you had hoped for.

But Jesus's anger in the temple didn't come from selfishness. Mark 11:17

says, "He said to them, 'The Scriptures declare, "My Temple will be called a house of prayer for all nations," but you have turned it into a den of thieves.'"

Jesus was angry because the temple was supposed to be a place for people to connect with God. They would pray, sing, and offer sacrifices for their sins. These merchants pretended to help the Israelites worship God, but really just wanted to make money. Jesus was angry because they were keeping people from God, and his whole purpose for being on earth was to bring people to God!

Sometimes anger can be controlled, but only when it comes from a heart of love, not a heart of selfishness. If you notice yourself getting angry a lot, ask God to show you if there's a selfish reason for your anger. If there is, ask him for a clean, unselfish heart and the power to be more like him.

DISCUSSION STARTER

- Name a time you've been angry recently. How might that anger have come out of selfishness? Let's bring that selfishness to God right now and ask for forgiveness.

PRAYER

God, please teach us to control our tempers. Help us to only get angry about things that make you angry. Amen.

DAY 97

CONTROLLING THE TONGUE

We can make a large horse go wherever we want by means of a
small bit in its mouth. And a small rudder makes a huge
ship turn wherever the pilot chooses to go, even though the
winds are strong. In the same way, the tongue is a
small thing that makes grand speeches.
But a tiny spark can set a great forest on fire. And among
all the parts of the body, the tongue is a flame of fire. It is a
whole world of wickedness, corrupting your entire body.
It can set your whole life on fire, for it is set on fire by hell itself.
(JAMES 3:3–6)

The little lantern with the little flame went unattended in the little barn, and
it unexpectedly got knocked over. Soon the barn was on fire. Then the shed
next door was ablaze. Within three days, that small lantern had burned over
seventeen thousand buildings, destroyed over three square miles of the city
of Chicago, killed three hundred people and left a hundred thousand homeless. Wow.

Sometimes small things can cause a lot of damage, like that little lantern
in the barn in the middle of Chicago.

Your tongue is one of those small things that can cause big problems. No,
your tongue won't start a literal fire, and it probably won't steal anything or
kill anyone. But here's what your tiny tongue can do: it can lie, call someone names, be rude and disrespectful, interrupt, yell, and be judgmental. Oh
dear, our tiny tongues can cause a lot of problems! That's why James said that
your tongue can set your whole life on fire. When we don't have self-control
over our words, we can ruin friendships, hurt our siblings, or land in the
principal's office.

Have you ever had this happen to you? You say something really disrespectful, and you want to smack your hands over your mouth because you can't believe you were that rude, but once you got started, your words were like a runaway horse, and you just couldn't stop being disrespectful. You didn't want to do it, but the words seemed to gallop past your brain and out your mouth.

That is called sin, but there is so much hope for you! You can't always be self-controlled, but Jesus came to be self-controlled for you. He works in you to keep your tongue from ruining your life with sinful words. The next time you feel your tongue start to get a little crazy, bite it (gently), and ask Jesus to help you control your words.

DISCUSSION STARTER

- How have you sinned with your words this week?
- Have you noticed me sinning with my words this week?

PRAYER

Jesus, we confess the many ways we have sinned with our words this week. We know it hurts others. Thank you for forgiving us. Please give us power to tame our tongues! Amen.

DAY 98

SWORD CONTROL

"Put your sword back in its place," Jesus said to him, "for all who draw the sword will die by the sword. Do you think I cannot call on my Father, and he will at once put at my disposal more than twelve legions of angels? But how then would the Scriptures be fulfilled that say it must happen in this way?"
(MATTHEW 26:52–54 NIV)

What do you know about fighting in an army? Maybe you know someone in the military, or you're in cadets or play a lot of army-based video games. Let me tell you about the army Israel was dealing with. At the time Jesus lived on earth, Rome was becoming a superpower in the Western world. They conquered all the land around the Mediterranean Sea, including North Africa, most of Europe, and the Middle East. They controlled this much land through their enormous army. If you were a regular foot soldier in the army, you would be part of a group called a *legion*. Each legion was made up of four thousand to six thousand soldiers.

So, when Jesus said he could immediately have more than twelve legions of angels at his side, he was talking about a massive army of angels—over fifty thousand angels!

Let's just say that Jesus had a *ton* of power. If I were about to get arrested and I had fifty thousand angels at my disposal, I'm not sure I would have the self-control to hold out my wrists and let them be tied up. (I guess it's a good thing I'm not Jesus!) What do you think would have happened if he had summoned his angel army? They would have obeyed, of course, because Jesus is their leader. They would have surrounded him and gotten rid of his enemies, and Jesus wouldn't have had to go through with the dying portion of his evening.

But Jesus had just spent a long time praying for God's will to be done, so he knew what had to happen next.

Instead of using the sword (or his angel army), Jesus chose to use the sword of the Spirit again. The Word of God had prophesied the Messiah would be arrested, killed, and raised from the dead, so he kept his cool and let the plan unfold.

As sinful humans, we're often guilty of drawing our swords instead of showing self-control. No, we don't have literal swords, but many things can hurt others just as much as swords. When we lose control and insult someone or treat someone different because of the color of their skin, we do just as much harm as slicing off someone's ear with a sword. We don't always know what God's will is, but we do know part of God's will: to love others. God will give you the self-control you need to love others like Jesus did.

Instead of living uncontrolled, let's let God teach us to live by the sword of the Spirit, which is the Word of God.

DISCUSSION STARTER

- If you had an angel army at your disposal, what would you do with it?
- Tell about a time when you lost control.

PRAYER

Thank you, Jesus, for being the perfect example of self-control. You know the situations where we lose control. Please help us live in your power instead of in our own power. Amen.

DAY 99

FEARLESS CONTROL

God has not given us a spirit of fear and timidity, but of power,
love, and self-discipline.
(2 TIMOTHY 1:7)

Have you ever been accused of something you didn't do? Maybe someone said you took the last cookie from the jar or accused you of cheating in a game. Maybe your mom thought you were lying when you were actually telling the truth, or your friend thought you said something mean about her.

It doesn't feel great to be accused of something we didn't do. That's a time when it can be super hard to have self-control. Normally we want to get angry with the person who's accused us, or get revenge, or sit in the corner and eat cheese.

Jesus was dragged to an illegal trial in the middle of the night. It was in the chief priest's home instead of a public place, and the leaders presented fake evidence against Jesus. They spit on him, beat him up, and made fun of him.

And what did Jesus do during this horrible trial? Mostly, he just stood there. I imagine temple guards holding their swords and spears in his face as he cocked his head, calmly listening to the charges. He spoke only once. Later, Jesus was also put on trial in front of the Jewish king named Herod, and Pilate, who represented the Romans in Israel. Jesus didn't lose his cool in front of them either.

Why did Jesus behave like this? Why didn't he defend himself, or fight back, or at least tell them they were missing the point? Well, Jesus told Pilate why when he said, "I was born and came into the world to testify to the truth" (John 18:37). Jesus knew there was a greater plan at work, and fighting wouldn't help. He is the perfect example of what Paul later wrote to his friend Timothy: "God has not given us a spirit of fear and timidity, but of power, love, and self-discipline." Jesus wasn't afraid. Instead, he was filled with power (because he knew exactly who he was), with love for his enemies, and with self-discipline.

Have you ever noticed that we tend to lose self-control when we're afraid? We're afraid of losing screen time, so we yell at our parents. We're afraid of looking weak in front of our friends, so we call another kid rude names. Or we're afraid of not getting enough supper, so we snatch up the last of the spaghetti.

Through Jesus, we can learn to have self-control in all those situations. He showed us that it's possible when we have his Spirit working inside our hearts.

DISCUSSION STARTER

- When do you tend to lose self-control? Do you think it's connected to fear? Why or why not?

PRAYER

Thank you, Jesus, for giving us a spirit of power, love, and self-discipline. Help us to live in that spirit instead of the spirit of fear. Amen.

DAY 100

THE POWERFUL SPIRIT

"Now I will send the Holy Spirit, just as my Father promised. But stay here in the city until the Holy Spirit comes and fills you with power from heaven."
(LUKE 24:49)

Do you have days where you wish God would make all the hard parts of your life go away? Wouldn't it be nice if he could make everything all better, so you never have to deal with a bully or spelling test or broken arm ever again?

Between Jesus's coming back to life and before he went back to heaven, his disciples were still a bit confused about what he had come to do. They thought he was going to kick out the Romans and make everything in Israel perfect. They really wanted all the hard stuff to stop too.

Jesus helped his friends understand what the purpose of his death and resurrection was. Then he gave them the perfect command: "Stay here in the city until the Holy Spirit comes and fills you with power from heaven." The disciples were (mostly) excited to tell everyone about what had happened, but they weren't fully equipped. They couldn't just bust down the doors of Jerusalem and start preaching. They needed something—or rather, Someone—first.

The disciples absolutely, totally, 100 percent needed the Holy Spirit. They needed him to help them speak God's truth to kings, and prisoners, and mobs who wanted to kill them. They needed him to help them serve the poor, the widows, and the orphans. They needed him to heal the lame and the blind and to raise up the dead.

You and I need the Holy Spirit too. Maybe you haven't had to face down a mob or preach to the President, but it might happen someday! And even if you don't do those things, God doesn't make all the hard stuff go away. There

SELF-CONTROL

will still be many reasons to need God through your life. The good news is, Jesus promised that "anyone who believes in me will do the same works I have done, and even greater works, because I am going to be with the Father" (John 14:12). That's because of the Holy Spirit living in us.

What a totally amazing promise! When you believe Jesus has died for your sins and given you his resurrection power through the Holy Spirit, you—yes, *you*—can do even greater works than him. Why? Because "the Spirit who lives in you is greater than the spirit who lives in the world" (1 John 4:4).

Just like the disciples, you absolutely, totally, 100 percent need the Holy Spirit. It's your choice whether or not you'll let him work in your life.

DISCUSSION STARTER

- Do you think the Holy Spirit is working in you? If so, how have you changed since we started reading this book?

PRAYER

God, you are absolutely, totally, 100 percent amazing, and we need you so much. Please help us see our need for you every day. Amen.

CONCLUSION

We've reached the final day of this devotional book! I can't believe we're all here. I needed an enormous amount of Holy Spirit help to write all these words, and you needed an enormous amount of Holy Spirit help to *read* all these words! Praise God!

Guess what? Your adventure in growing in the fruit of the Spirit doesn't stop here. You'll be growing in the fruit of the Spirit your whole life. The longer you follow God, the more you'll act like him.

Following God and letting him grow the fruit of the Spirit in you might take you on some wild adventures. God has helped me grow in love and joy as he helps me love people who are different from me. He helped me grow in peace even during some very sad times in my life. God helps me with patience and self-control every day I spend as a mom (and I'm sure my kids are growing in patience every day they live with me too). He helped me grow in kindness and goodness when he led me to donate a kidney to a perfect stranger. And God helped me grow in faithfulness by reminding me to sit in my chair every day and write this book for you. Your adventures won't be the same as mine, but I know God is going to take the life you give him and do amazing things with it.

May Christ make his home in your hearts as you trust in him.

May your roots grow down into God's love and keep you strong.

And may you have the power to understand, as all God's people should, how wide, how long, how high, and how deep his love is.

May you experience the love of Christ, though it is too great to understand fully.

Then you will be made complete with all the fullness of life and power that comes from God.

—Adapted from Ephesians 3:17–19

ACKNOWLEDGMENTS

As always, my biggest and forever thanks goes to God. Thank you, Father, for creating me; thank you, Jesus, for being the author and perfector of my faith; and thank you, Holy Spirit, for guiding me and growing me (way too slowly at times) in the fruit of the Spirit.

Next in line is my husband, who granted me many evenings holed up in my office so I could write this for you all, and my boys for letting me test out devotions on them. Jon, Ethan, Oliver, and Jackson, here's to you. Let's have a picnic in the park to celebrate!

My critique partners have been absolute saints this year, helping me untangle gnarly theological thoughts and inspiring me with illustrations and ideas month after month. Bethany Den Boer, Belinda Grimbeek, Laura Ann Miller, Nicole Schrader, and Susan Simpson, you make me a better writer. A big thanks to Karen Neumair for believing in this book from the start and finding it the perfect home. Finally, Janyre Tromp, thanks for pushing me to dig deeper and keep polishing. This book is far more delightful and practical because of you.